MARKETING FOR RAINMAKERS

MARKETING FOR RAINMAKERS

52 Rules of Engagement to Attract and Retain Customers for Life

PHIL FRAGASSO

WILEY

John Wiley & Sons, Inc.

Published by John Wiley & Sons, Inc., Hoboken, New Jersey.
Published simultaneously in Canada.

For general information on our other products and services or for technical support, please contact our Customer Care Department within the United States at (800) 762-2974, outside the United States at (317) 572-3993 or fax (317) 572-4002.

Wiley also publishes its books in a variety of electronic formats. Some content that appears in print may not be available in electronic books. For more information about Wiley products, visit our Web site at www.wiley.com.

Library of Congress Cataloging-in-Publication Data:

Fragasso, Philip M., 1950-
    Marketing for rainmakers : 52 rules of engagement to attract and retain customers for life / Phil Fragasso.
        p.   cm.
    Includes bibliographical references and index.
    ISBN 978-0-470-24753-2 (cloth)
        1. Customer relations.   2. Customer services.   3. Marketing.   I. Title.
HF5415.5.F68   2008
658.8—dc22

2008002740

Printed in the United States of America

10 9 8 7 6 5 4 3 2 1

For Laura Marie
My Rainmaking Soulmate

Contents

CONTENTS

Contents

CONTENTS

ACKNOWLEDGMENTS

The person most responsible for *Marketing for Rainmakers*, as it exists today, is my literary agent, Michael Snell. Michael is a rare breed. I approached him unannounced and he took me under his wing—freely giving of his time and attention, with no guarantee that his efforts would be rewarded. Michael has been a delight to work with, and I look forward to thanking him in future volumes.

So much of what I know and believe about marketing grew out of the relationships I had with colleagues at Wang, Honeywell, Sun Life Financial, Columbia Funds, and Rydex Investments. I have been blessed to work with many highly creative, energetic people who continually amazed me with their insight and commitment.

My business partner, Jane Mancini, is a rainmaker without peer. We have worked together on three different occasions, and I never fail to learn from her, laugh with her, and blaze new trails with her. Had I never met Jane, this book would never have been written.

Matt Holt's team at John Wiley & Sons, Inc., has been a model of efficiency and support. Jessica Campilango, Christine Moore, and Kate Lindsay have helped and advised at every stage of editing and production, and have done so with personality and humor.

And then, of course, we come to my family. There are few joys in life equal to watching your children grow and discover themselves. My son and daughter, Michael and Julia, have brought smiles and made us proud countless times in countless ways.

The woman in my life also deserves credit—not just for this book, but for putting up with my somewhat idiosyncratic ways. Laura is a partner in the fullest sense of the word and contributes greatly to everything I have accomplished and, as she is wont to point out, everything I have screwed up. It was love at first sight, and it remains so today.

Introduction

Making Rain While the Sun Shines

In a world where even brain surgery isn't as hard as it used to be, marketing remains sheathed in mystery. And who's to blame for that? Marketers. As a group, marketers tend to be overwrought, shamelessly self-indulgent, and off-the-charts in self-aggrandizement and self-importance. And I ought to know, because I've been one of them for over twenty-five years.

On the rainmaking side of the equation, there exists broad consensus that rainmaking is a divine gift. It is present at birth, and no amount of familial or professional nurturing can make it blossom if the seed wasn't planted at conception. It is a genetic predisposition not unlike Tom Brady's arm, Tracy Chapman's voice, and Nicole Kidman's face.

Except it's all hogwash.

Marketing is simple, and rainmaking can be taught and learned. Put it all together and you've got the best of all worlds—rainmaker marketing, the Holy Grail of the business world. Let's begin the quest by looking at the two components (marketing and rainmaking) and then discovering how the whole (rainmaker marketing) is far greater than the sum of the parts.

MARKETING

Over the years, marketers have embraced—or had thrust upon them—many definitions of their craft. The textbook definition—which is still taught today in some of our most hallowed halls—distills marketing down to the 4Ps: product, price, place, and promotion. In addition to being annoyingly alliterative, this four-part litany is simplistic to the point of being meaningless. It also omits the two most important Ps of all—passion and people. The bottom line is that regardless of whether the 4Ps ever had any relevance to effective marketing—they don't today. They'll only slow you down, hold you down, and keep you down.

Back in the 1970s and '80s, marketing's buzz phrase was to "sell the sizzle, not the steak." Compared to the 4Ps, this definition was a stroke of genius (though, strangely enough, still too alliterative for most tastes). This line of thinking acknowledged that there was a lot more to the product than the product itself. It understood that most purchases were based on emotion—not logic. It raised concepts like perception vs. reality—where perception was the brand and reality was the product. And it pointed out that people were buying the perception (i.e., the brand) while most companies remained insistent on selling the reality (i.e., the product). Notwithstanding its good intentions, the "sell the sizzle" concept is a bit too glib and too focused on the immediately gratifying elements of marketing. It grew out of a short-sighted and short-term approach to marketing designed to grow top-line sales with little regard for the bottom-line growth that only a long-term relationship can bring. In simplest terms, "sell the sizzle" is a one-night stand while rainmaker marketing is a marriage.

There are lots of other definitions of marketing that have been bandied about over the years, but none of them gets to the heart of the matter. Marketing, when you distill its myriad facets down to the core, is focused on one thing and one thing only—*motivating*. Good marketing should be designed to motivate some*one* to do some*thing*. It should be a call to action—a call to action with a real sense of urgency to it.

So if marketing equals motivating—who's being motivated and what are they being motivated to do? Well it depends on what business you're in, but there are typically three audiences that need to be motivated—employees, distributors, and customers.

Employees

Employees need to be motivated to achieve their personal best every day in everything they do. CEOs from every industry and every size company wax poetic about how their people are their most valuable asset. And while these well-meaning, and occasionally sincere, sentiments may have a short-term impact on employee morale, they do nothing to truly motivate the rank-and-file. Why? Because there's no spark. There's nothing to capture the imagination. There's nothing to feel—other than an avuncular pat on the head. There's no cause and effect, and there's no call to action. Which is precisely where the marketer comes in. His or her job is to bring the CEO's platitudes to life. In short, it's the marketer's job to make employees *feel* like the company's most valuable asset and feel good about themselves *because* they're associated with the company.

A good way to understand this is to equate the employment contract to the marriage contract. Assuming you're married, think about your first date with your spouse. Think about your first kiss, your first intimate encounter, your engagement, wedding, and honeymoon. If you were like most people deeply in love, you looked forward to every moment with your life partner. You pledged to love her more every day, and you promised that your actions would serve to make her love you more every day as well. Now think back to your first day working for a new company and a new boss. Didn't you have that same level of excitement (sans the raging hormonal urges of romance)? Didn't you dive into your new responsibilities with energy and enthusiasm? Weren't you determined to prove that the best man for the job had indeed been hired?

And in both cases—in marriage and at work—what happened after a few months or years? Did your spouse fall or get knocked off her pedestal? Did your boss morph into a less-than-ideal role model or mentor? Did love-making and dinnertime conversations acquire a certain sameness to them? Did your job responsibilities become repetitive and pointless?

What changed? Probably not the core elements of your marriage or job. In most cases, what changed is you—a change which is far more convenient to ascribe to your spouse or boss. And the cause of the change is a lack of motivation. The thrill of the chase is gone. The shine has worn off.

So what does this have to do with marketing? Well, similar to a marriage counselor, it's the marketer's job to continually remind the employee why he chose to join XYZ Company in the first place. It's the marketer's job to paint a picture of what lies ahead and create a compelling storyline that the employee will want to experience and help write. In work and in marriage, we feel best about those relationships that make us feel good about ourselves. It's a key ingredient of marketing to make employees feel good—and in return they'll work doubly hard to ensure that the company does well.

Distributors

Distributors—whether new business developers, account executives, wholesalers, sales representatives (salaried or commissioned), independent brokers, retailers, or clerks—must be motivated on a continual basis. Strong distribution is critical in today's marketplace—and strong distributors are heavily courted by the competition. It's the marketer's responsibility to ensure that his distributors understand his company's story (often referred to as a value proposition or brand position), feel part of it, and believe in it.

And how do you accomplish that? Well certainly not by staying in your office and talking to other home office types. Marketers need to get out into the field. Learn what works and what doesn't work. Talk to top producers and ferret out the secret of their success. Talk to mid- and low-level producers and determine what they need to move up to the next level. Simply demonstrating that you're willing to listen is a motivational tool in itself, but the key is to use this information-gathering exercise to develop marketing tools and programs designed specifically to help your producers grow their business and work smarter.

There's nothing more motivating in life than knowing someone has your best interests in mind. Sales and marketing have a *quid pro quo* relationship. Have your distributors do well by you, and you'll do well by them.

Customers

There are actually two types of customers who need to be motivated. The first group is obvious and relatively easy—your prospective customers. You simply have to motivate them to learn about your product or service, make them believe it will satisfy a core need, and prompt them to initiate a relationship by making the purchase. At the risk of taking the marriage analogy a bit too far, consider the fact that it's a whole lot easier to fall in love while dating than it is to stay in love when the kids are wailing, the sink is full, and bills are piling up. Similarly, it's fairly easy to convince an audience geared towards excess consumption that your product or service will satisfy their every need and provide the answer to the question they never even thought to ask.

Once you've delivered the solution, however, the hard part begins. That's when the relationship begins and your motivational program has to kick into high gear. The smoke-and-mirror motivational techniques that opened the door won't work any more. You've got to deliver on your brand promise, identify additional needs, and wow the customer in every interaction. The goal is to so engage the customer that when the competition sashays into his life, flaunting its attractive features and benefits, he won't even entertain the idea of straying. He's become a brand monogamist—and you've become the envy of every marketer in the land.

RAINMAKING

Rainmaking typically refers to the ability of certain employees to bring in high volumes of new business and new clients. It is most commonly associated with professional services firms, especially law practices. In reality, rainmakers operate in all fields and industries, in all size companies, and at every level of the corporate hierarchy.

Rainmaking, as with marketing, is often confused with selling but, at its core, has considerably more depth and substance. Selling connotes a transaction, while rainmaking implies a consultative relationship. Selling pushes while rainmaking pulls. Rainmakers love what they do and believe fervently that they are delivering a service of immense value. They have a long-term strategy and vision, view themselves as problem solvers, and genuinely enjoy the people they work with. The workday is not something to get through; it is a series of personal interactions to be relished.

Most importantly, rainmaking is not about the product; it's about making connections between client needs and the most appropriate products and solutions. That's why there are some universal principles that guide rainmaker's success regardless of their specific field or specialty. And that's why this book exists.

The book also exists because rainmakers are in short supply where they are needed most—in smaller businesses run by professional service providers (e.g., attorneys, architects, consultants, engineers, accountants, real estate brokers, financial planners, graphic designers, massage therapists, executive recruiters, physicians, and a host of other highly skilled independent entrepreneurs). The dearth of rainmakers in professional services firms derives from the widespread belief among professionals that selling is dirty and beneath them. They resist and reject any activity that even hints of selling. Notwithstanding the aforementioned fact that rainmaking and selling are not the same, this pervasive belief severely limits the growth prospects for otherwise sound businesses.

Rainmaker Marketing

So if marketing's goal is to motivate and rainmaking's focus is on building relationships, then rainmaker marketing should be all about motivating the target audience to enter into a deep-seated relationship with the company, brand, product, or service that's being offered. A relationship which will experience a variety of ups-and-downs, but which will be so *engaging* in the fullest sense of the word (i.e., captivating, involving, charming, engrossing, interlocking, and betrothing) that it can withstand the test of time and serve as an advocate for new relationships. That's the best you can hope for from any customer relationship—and that's precisely where *Marketing for Rainmakers* is designed to lead.

Rainmaker marketing is a 24/7 endeavor. It's not something you do at work. It's not a department or a business function. Rather, it represents and reflects the way you live your life. It's both aspirational and inspirational.

Rainmaking marketers possess an internal drive to succeed regardless of external factors. They don't sit back and wait for the perfect scenario to arrive before practicing their business-building magic. They make the most of every opportunity. They approach all aspects of their business—branding, strategic planning, tactical execution, customer relations, and competitive analysis—with the same hardwired dedication to building relationships that can last a lifetime.

Technically and intellectually, rainmaking marketers tend towards the average. What sets them apart is their mindset. They think differently and, as a result, act differently, see things differently, and are perceived differently. And as Robert Frost advised, when two roads diverge they take the one less traveled. It makes for a fun and interesting journey. So let's begin.

Section One

THE BRAND-FOCUSED
RAINMAKING MARKETER

ROE #1

BEGIN AT THE END

The best advice I ever got in my career was that I needed to begin at the end. I needed to visualize my legacy. Most people associate a legacy with the transfer of worldly possessions from one generation to the next. So it's not a great leap to realize that each of us also create professional legacies that we leave to the next-generation marketers and rainmakers of our company, brand, or product line. The key is to define that legacy—determine exactly what it is that you want to accomplish, and then focus all your time and energy on making it a reality.

This concept of a visualized legacy is focused on defining and achieving goals. And it gets at the heart of what successful marketing is all about. In today's business world, every marketing dollar needs to be accounted for and needs to provide a clear return on its investment. Every single marketing program—whether advertising, public relations, client seminars, promotional mailings—needs to be goal-oriented. Marketing needs to have a payoff. If it doesn't create additional revenue,

3

boost profits, reduce costs of acquisition, or enhance customer loyalty—in other words, if it doesn't motivate people to take actions that will directly contribute to growing your business—then it's simply not worth doing. Your job is to visualize precisely what action you want people to take.

Visualization is usually associated with athletes—particularly peak performers. Baseball players picture themselves hitting a home run, sprinters see themselves bursting over the finish line ahead of the pack, and gymnasts see themselves performing a perfect routine and sticking the landing to a standing ovation. The process works the same for rainmakers and marketers. Architects visualize their design, fully constructed, with people walking through the doors and gliding up the escalators. Attorneys see themselves in the courtroom with the judge and jury hanging on their every word. And marketers of every stripe see their efforts ringing the cash register.

Like all things, visualization does not come easy. It requires practice. Visualization is far different than simply saying "I think I can, I think I can." It involves images rather than words and narration. And the more vivid the image—the more detailed and nuanced—the more impact it will have on the skills that you're trying to sharpen.

A Lesson from the Greatest Rainmaker of All-Time

Thomas Watson, Sr. became general manager of the Computing Tabulating Recording Corporation (CTR) in 1914. At the time, CTR was a manufacturer of automatic meat slicers, weighing scales, and punched card equipment. The company had fewer than 400 employees, but Watson had big plans for the small company and, in 1924, he renamed it International Business Machines.

Watson's description of his thought processes and game plan for the company is far too powerful to paraphrase. So here, in Watson's own words, is the secret of his personal and professional success:

> IBM is what it is today for three special reasons. The first reason is that, at the very beginning, I had a very clear picture of what the company would look like when it was finally done. You might say I had a model in my mind of what it would look like when the dream—my vision—was in place.
>
> The second reason was that once I had that picture, I then asked myself how a company which looked like that would have to act. I then created a picture of how IBM would act when it was finally done.
>
> The third reason IBM has been so successful was that once I had a picture of how IBM would look like when the dream was in place and how such a company would have to act, I then realized that, unless we began to act that way from the very beginning, we would never get there.
>
> In other words, I realized that for IBM to become a great company it would have to act like a great company long before it ever became one.
>
> From the very outset, IBM was fashioned after the template of my vision. And each and every day we attempted to model the company after that template. At the end of each day, we asked ourselves how well we did, and discovered the disparity between where we were and where we had committed ourselves to be, and, at the start of the following day, set out to make up for the difference.
>
> Every day at IBM was a day devoted to business development, not doing business.
>
> We didn't do business at IBM, we built one.

Thomas Watson, Sr. didn't invent the concept of visualization but he embraced it with a fervor that should be an inspiration to us all. Interestingly, it would be very easy to reword Watson's quote and replace "IBM" with your own name or the name of your company. To wit:

> Thirty years from now, I will have achieved all that I am capable of for three special reasons. The first reason is that, starting today, I have a very clear picture of what a successful career will look and feel like when I retire.
>
> The second reason is that now that I have that picture, I can ask myself how a successful career like that would have to be built. I can then create a picture of how I would have to act and interact to achieve that goal.
>
> The third reason I will have been so successful is that once I had a picture of what my career would look like when the dream was in place and how I would have to act, I realized that, unless I began to act that way from this day forward, I would never get there.
>
> In other words, I realize today that for me to become a great rainmaker I would have to act like a great rainmaker long before I ever became one.
>
> From the very outset, my career was fashioned after the template of my vision. And each and every day I attempted to model myself after that template. At the end of each day, I would ask myself how well I had done, and discovered the disparity between where I was and where I had committed myself to be, and, at the start of the following day, I set out to make up for the difference.

A COROLLARY LESSON FROM SOMEONE WHO WOULDN'T QUALIFY TO HOLD TOM WATSON'S MEMORY STICK

Several years ago, I headed marketing for a mid-size investment company that had aspirations of growing substantially larger. In establishing our marketing strategy, we focused on the

corporate vision of being a top-tier investment company.
We started by considering what our larger brethren looked like.
Using that approach, we made four generalizations about
these firms:

1. They were well known

2. They had positive reputations

3. They had several "category killer" products and/or specialties

4. They were sold through a vast army of financial advisors

The next step was to translate these four attributes of top-tier
companies into the primary strategies that the marketing group
would pursue to support the corporate goal. Specifically:

- Increase Awareness – articulate the corporate story in a way
  that is engaging and compelling

- Focus on Education – Become the go-to resource for financial
  advisors and individual investors to learn about alternative
  investment strategies

- Seize Opportunities – Capitalize on the increasing interest in
  alternative investments by focusing on our industry-leading
  suite of synthetic hedge fund products

- Drive Activity – Attract new advisors, encourage existing
  producers to place additional assets with us, and develop an
  easy-to-implement referral program

A good exercise would be to follow this same structure
and assess what your own aspirational role models look like.
Extrapolating from them, you can then outline specific steps
you can take today to move you closer to your goal.

A Corollary Lesson from My Inner "Dr. Phil"

Life is short—which is why we should always kiss our spouses goodbye, tell our kids we love them at every opportunity, and make sure our friends know how important they are to us.

Our professional lives are equally short. So focus on what's most important. Do the right thing at the right time. And always keep the end in sight—it's nearer than any of us ever wants to admit.

ROE #2

BE A HOBGOBLIN

You know the old adage about consistency being the hobgoblin of little minds? Well toss it into the trash alongside the 4Ps. Consistency is paramount in building powerful brands, developing effective marketing programs, and maintaining lifelong relationships with your customers.

Think about the two or three companies (or, if you prefer, brands or products) that—from a marketing perspective—you most admire. Whether they're manufacturers, retailers, or service providers, I'd bet the price of this book that the thing they all have in common—and the element that drives your admiration—is consistency. Consistency in message. Consistency in look, feel, and tone. Consistency in quality.

Consistency is the hallmark of a truly integrated marketing program. Indeed, it's the cornerstone of the building-block philosophy that is at the heart of each ROE. Every element of your marketing program needs to relate to every other element. Every brochure (advertisement, web site, mailer, trade show booth, press release, blog) needs to build off the foundation of what came before and needs to serve as a springboard for whatever comes next.

It sounds easy, but consistency requires commitment and hard work. Many larger companies even have a formal "Brand Champion" to ensure that everything the customer sees or hears is "on brand"—communicating a single message that never wavers from their core positioning.

The lack of consistency that afflicts most marketing programs usually derives from three sources:

1. A misinterpretation of Marshall McLuhan's dictum that "the medium is the message." In today's world, it's the message (and the look, feel, and tone that comprise that message) that's critical—not the medium. A common mistake of marketers is to be consistent within a given medium but inconsistent across media.

2. Outwardly driven impatience. Even the best marketing programs can't always deliver immediate results—so there's often pressure (usually from one's sales colleagues) to try a different tack.

3. Inwardly driven impatience. Because marketers live with their brand 24/7, and because they tend to be creative types, they often get tired of their message (and its accompanying look, feel, and tone) long before their audience even has a chance to be fully engaged by it.

Like all virtues, consistency requires dedication, but it also pays huge dividends. So the next time you're tempted to take the easy route towards inconsistency, aim a bit higher and be the hobgoblin that your company or brand deserves.

THE BEST OF THE HOBGOBLINS

Consistency in positioning is critical to the success of any enterprise and to an individual's personal brand as well. There are many businesses, organizations, and individuals that do abide by the Hobgoblin ROE, and a closer look at three disparate examples provides valuable insight on how consistency can be applied in a variety of ways from a variety of platforms:

- The Marine Corps – Despite being the smallest of the U.S. military services, the Marines are the most well known and highly regarded. As an organization and a team, the Marines are also the quintessential exemplars of consistency. Current and former Marines begin or end almost every communication with their long-standing motto, *"Semper Fi."* There are few Americans who could not correctly fill in the blank when asked to complete this tagline: "The Few. The Proud. The_____." Most importantly, however, the Marines stand for something— and that something never wavers. Marines are tough, disciplined, and loyal. They arrive first and leave last. And most importantly, they are men and women of character. They view themselves as Marines, and fervently believe that "Once a Marine, Always a Marine." None of this happened overnight. It was the result of a clear vision and a consistently applied approach to their business (whether keeping the peace or fighting a war). The Marine Corps brand did not flourish because of words—it became a living breathing organization because of its actions. Character is not a result of what you say, it's a reflection of what you do consistently.

- McDonald's – One of the most recognizable brands in the world, McDonald's has been a picture of consistency from its very beginnings. In fact, McDonald's has been described as the best restaurant in the world—not because of the food quality, but because of the consistency of the overall experience. Like the strongest brands (Coca-Cola, Harley-Davidson, Apple, and Starbucks come to mind), our impression of McDonald's is the result of myriad interactions with its iconic Golden Arches, Big Macs, Happy Meals, and Ronald McDonald. Purists might argue that McDonald's has not been true to their brand due to the introduction of non-hamburger products like chicken and salads, but those folks are missing the core positioning that McDonald's has adhered to for over fifty years. McDonald's was never a "hamburger joint." Rather the company offered a convenient and affordable venue for a family meal or snack—and while they have greatly expanded their menu, they have not wavered from their original guiding principle.

- Richard Branson – With a net worth of over $2 billion, Richard Branson is one of the richest and most powerful businesspeople in the world. He runs the Virgin Group conglomerate of some 350 companies—most of which he has founded personally. His business interests run from airlines and music to cell phones and bridal shops, and he has been criticized for overextending the Virgin brand just to please his own ego. Branson sees it otherwise. He's been quoted as saying, "In the beginning it was just about the business—now it's about the brand." And the brand, in truth, is as much Branson himself as it is Virgin. Branson is a control freak—which is a key component of consistency—but he also has a reputation for empowering his employees. Most importantly, he is passionate about ensuring that he and Virgin stand for something real and meaningful—in particular, a risk-taking, establishment-challenging, and edgy approach to life and business. This approach is so consistently woven through everything that Branson touches that it is

highlighted front-and-center on the Virgin Group web site.
To wit:

Our role is to be the consumer champion, and we do this by
delivering to our brand values, which are: Value for Money, Good
Quality, Brilliant Customer Service, Innovative, Competitively
Challenging, and Fun. Richard Branson set out with these
principles in mind in the 1970s and they still really define what
Virgin is all about. Most companies in the world have a set of
brand values, which in a lot of cases can be completely
meaningless. Virgin believes that the most important thing is
the way those values are delivered and brought to life. Here are
some examples of the ways that Virgin delivers its brand values:

Value for Money

Simple, honest & transparent pricing—not necessarily the
cheapest on the market (e.g. Virgin Blue Australia—low cost
airlines with transparent pricing)

Good Quality

High standards, attention to detail, being honest and delivering on
promises (e.g. Virgin Atlantic Upper Class Suite—limousine
service, lounge, large flat bed on board, freedom menu, etc.,)

Innovation

Challenging convention with big and little product service ideas;
innovative, modern and stylish design (e.g. Virgin Trains new
pendolino—fast tilting train with shop, radio, digital seat
reservations, and new sleek design)

BRILLIANT CUSTOMER SERVICE

Friendly, human & relaxed; professional but uncorporate
(e.g. Virgin Mobile UK which has won awards for its customer
service, treats its customers as individuals, and pays out staff
bonuses according to customer satisfaction survey results.)

COMPETITIVELY CHALLENGING

Sticking two fingers up to the establishment and fighting the big
boys—usually with a bit of humour (e.g. Virgin Atlantic
successfully captured the public spirit by taking on British Airways'
dirty tricks openly—and winning. Later, advertising messages such
as "BA Don't Give A Shiatsu" both mocked BA and delivered a
positive message about the airline's service.)

FUN

Every company in the world takes itself seriously so we think it's
important that we provide the public and our customers with a bit
of entertainment (e.g. VAA erected a sign over the BA-sponsored,
late-finishing London Eye saying: BA Can't Get It Up. [In
addition] Virgin Cola's launch in USA saw Richard drive a tank
down 5th Avenue and then "blow up" the Coke sign in Times
Square, mocking the "cola wars")

You have to love the fact that Virgin includes actual examples
to bring their corporate values to life. And while that may
seem like a little thing, it further demonstrates consistency in
communicating their brand and positioning. A list of generic
values like "fun" and "innovation" would be meaningless in
isolation. I have personally worked for several stodgy companies
that considered themselves to be innovative and fun loving—but

I've never known a CEO who would dare to strip down to a nude bodysuit, hover above New York's Times Square, and cover his private parts with a Virgin cell phone to promote the launch of Virgin Mobile USA. That's the sort of thing Richard Branson does consistently—and why he is a hobgoblin par excellence.

ROE #3

GET YOURSELF SOME CULTURE

Be honest. Would you have answered this ad?

MEN WANTED for hazardous journey. Small wages, Bitter cold, long months of complete Darkness, constant Danger, safe return Doubtful. Honor and Recognition in case of success.

Sir Ernest Shackleton attracted five-thousand applicants for his expedition to the South Pole via this apocryphal ad. Shackleton knew exactly the type of man he was looking for, and the stakes were too high to settle for less. He had a vision of what he wanted to achieve, and he required a supporting cast that shared that vision. As for the men who responded, it would be hard to imagine any weak-kneed whiners among them. Shackleton was passionate about surrounding himself with like-minded individuals of character and fortitude so that, when the going got really tough, everyone would stay focused on the larger goal and keep driving ahead.

Take another look at the ad and you'll see there is absolutely no mention of specific skill sets or experience. Shackleton was following the approach used by today's college football coaches to "recruit the athlete not the position." High school quarterbacks are routinely switched to wide receivers and cornerbacks in order to play at the college level. They're recruited for their athleticism and then taught how to play the specified position.

Every organization needs a Shackleton and, in an ideal world, it would be the rainmakers who serve as coaches and act as role models. Their first job would be to create and maintain a marketing culture throughout the company. All employees, regardless of title or function, would view themselves as marketers—and view every interaction with every customer as a marketing opportunity not to be wasted. Whether it's a customer service person handling the setup of a new account, a finance person explaining an invoice, a receptionist taking a message, or an IT person evaluating new voicemail systems, everyone should understand that they are representing the total enterprise, they have the opportunity to delight or disappoint, and they contribute to both the top and bottom lines.

This boils down to the key point that marketing is not a department. Rather, it is a mindset, a way of viewing the total business from the client's perspective. The development of this enterprise-wide mindset begins at the hiring and training stage of new employees and associates.

Of all the things you do to build your business, the hiring process is probably the most important. Hiring is a crapshoot and it's very hard to get rid of people once they're on the payroll. People who interview well may end up being psychos, complainers, or plain incompetents once on the job. Your organization represents a living breathing organism, and the last thing you ever want to do is introduce a cancer that can eat away at your efforts from the inside out. That's why you—as the rainmaking and marketing heart-and-soul of the organization—need to be actively involved in the recruiting, interviewing, orientation, and training of new employees. That may seem like a lot to ask, as these would not be billable hours and would represent time that could be "better spent" prospecting, gaining new skills, or strengthening relationships with existing clients. But think back to Shackleton and ask yourself whether his time would have been better spent evaluating equipment or studying maps rather than building a team that would help ensure the success of his mission. You're also working on an important mission, and your team will have a major impact—positive or negative—on accomplishing it.

Here are some ways to build and maintain a rainmaker-marketing culture:

- Never be afraid to hire people who are, or have the potential to be, better than you. That's the mistake weak leaders make— trying to ensure that they remain the alpha dog. Instead, hire people who would be legitimate contenders for your job. They'll make you better and make the organization better.

- Don't hire people who say they expect to be in the same position in three to five years. Ambition is a sign of intelligence, enthusiasm, and commitment. Hire people who are restless, rather than those who simply want to rest.

- Be specific in your expectations. Everyone in your organization should have a set of clear, written objectives that are achievable but also represent a stretch. These objectives should be arrived at collaboratively rather than being imposed, and should encompass personal development as well as professional growth.

- Be specific in your rewards. While a pat on the back or an unexpected bonus for a job well done can be great ways to let people know they're appreciated, you'll get a lot more mileage from specificity. Rewarding specific behaviors will reinforce those behaviors and send a clear message to the rest of the organization.

- Be inclusive. Good ideas can come from anywhere in the organization, so give everyone a voice at the table and an opportunity to utilize and demonstrate their creativity. The voice of every employee is unique—just as it is with your clients.

- Break down walls. Silos should only exist on farms. Foster an environment of cross-fertilization with minimal hierarchy. Rainmakers are highly entrepreneurial and their organizations should reflect that. Nurture a start-up mentality in which everyone is agile, flexible, poised for action, and in it for each other's mutual success.

- Create employee evangelists. Much had been written about the mindset of customers as they move up the loyalty ladder—progressing from suspects to prospects to customers to clients to evangelists. There is a similar progression in how individuals feel about their work lives. At the bottom rung are workers who view their job as a paycheck, and at the top rung are the corporate evangelists who love what they do, believe in the product they offer, delight in delighting their customers, and are walking-talking PR machines for your firm.

- Communicate consistently, continually, and credibly. As you build a high-performing team, it's essential to keep everyone informed. Reinforce your vision and ensure a common understanding of long-term strategies and short-term tactics. Explain what you're doing and why you're doing it—not for approval, but rather to help ensure buy-in. Remember that failure to communicate is the number one reason why relationships—from marital to professional—fail.

- Be fearless. Success happens when people lose the fear of failure. Nurture a confidence in exploring new ideas and trying new approaches. Sure, mistakes will be made; but very little of importance is ever achieved without taking a risk. Demonstrate that you are willing to accept responsibility for your own mistakes and work hard to learn from them, and your colleagues and staff will do the same.

- Throw down gauntlets. People respond to challenges better than orders and mandates. Personal pride in achievement is a great motivator, as is being part of a team focused on a common goal.

- Articulate success. People who know what success looks like and feels like are far more likely to achieve it. The "keep your eye on the prize" adage gets its power from the belief that if you can see it, you can reach it. Just as marathon runners get an extra shot of adrenalin when the finish line is in sight, your staff and colleagues will remain motivated when success seems real and just around the corner.

Your success in building a marketing-oriented culture will have palpable impact on your firm's dealings with clients. Enthusiasm will be rampant and contagious; quality will improve as everyone understands their role in the business continuum of attracting and retaining customers; and your job will be made infinitely easier as everyone will be on the same page.

And what, specifically, would total success at building a marketing culture look like? It would be a group of individuals who respect the particular skills and experience that each brings to the table, who share a vision, push themselves to succeed, and believe wholeheartedly in Vince Lombardi's credo that, "If you are not fired with enthusiasm, you will be fired with enthusiasm."

ROE #4

BE TRUE TO YOUR SCHOOL

Remember the passion and excitement of high school pep rallies and homecoming games? Remember how you believed—in your heart of hearts—that your school was truly second to none? Your passion served two purposes: it helped motivate the athletic team to deliver its best performance, and it made you feel like part of something much larger. As every successful rainmaker will attest, it's a lot easier to sell a product that you believe in than one that simply puts dollars in your pocket. Passion sells. Enthusiasm serves to enthuse. And passionate enthusiasm is the most engaging and persuasive force known to the rainmaking universe.

It boils down to the difference between knowing your business and loving your business—a difference that will be readily apparent to your clients, colleagues, and staff members. While I've heard that the climactic aspects of love can sometimes be faked, truly passionate love must be authentic or it will ring sadly hollow. The first order of rainmaker marketing, then, is to choose a field, product, or specialty that truly interests, fascinates, and energizes you. Most often that will mean a field, product, or specialty that you believe contributes to the greater good. If you truly believe you are adding value through your work, you will make the life-altering transformation from being a worker to an evangelist. You view your work as a mission, you believe your words because you live them yourself everyday, and you feel sad when clients choose a competitive offering because they won't experience the benefits that only you can deliver. If it all sounds cult-like, that's because it is. Many of the greatest corporate successes of the past and present have enjoyed cult-like loyalty among employees and customers. In the past, that list included firms like IBM, Disney, and Merck. Today, the list includes Apple, Starbucks, FedEx, and Target. The common element among these diverse corporate entities translates to an evangelist-like belief that they were doing the right thing for the right reasons. Sure they were making gobs of money, but that was the byproduct of what they viewed as their core mission.

Going back to the high school pep rally analogy, think about the basis of your excitement and passion. While you might have had a favorite player or a particularly hated rival, your dedication to the team had much more to do with a feeling of vicarious belonging and the belief that you too were contributing to a victory. You truly believed that the harder you cheered the harder the athletes would play and the more likely victory would become. And there's a lot of truth to that. Home field advantage is a widely accepted and verifiable aspect of college-level and professional sports. In fact, Las Vegas oddsmakers typically add an extra two or three points to the home team when setting the point spread in football games. That also explains why sports fans live and die with their beloved teams. They see themselves as being on the field with their heroes, blocking, tackling, and talking trash. When their team wins, they relish the victory;

and when the team falls to defeat, they feel beaten as well. The most effective salespeople, marketers, and rainmakers experience similar feelings of euphoria and anguish as their professional efforts succeed or fail.

Rainmaking is built upon a strong foundation of interpersonal relationships based on mutual trust and mutual interests. Logic plays a part, but emotional connections rule the day. Let me share a personal example that occurred over twenty years ago yet still remains vivid in my memory. I was selling my home and invited several real estate agents to view the house and submit proposals for the listing. Now there is no single financial transaction with stronger emotional implications than the process of selling one's home; and so I paid close attention to every word, nuance, and facial tic that might provide a hint of each agent's true character and feelings. The first few agents were uniformly business-like and pointed out things that should be fixed, provided their view of current market conditions, and quoted fair asking prices. Another one took the same business-like approach, but I heard something extra in the tone of his voice and saw something comforting in his body language. He truly loved what he was doing and especially enjoyed working with older homes like mine. He genuinely liked its quirky character, appreciated the renovations we had done, and saw the potential that new owners could further enjoy. His contract, commission, and recommended listing price were in line with his competitors; but he won the business because he was focused not on selling a house but on finding a new owner who would love the wainscoted, albeit slightly askew, pantry as much as he and I did. He had turned a transactional relationship into a team effort, and we entered into a personal partnership that was to our mutual benefit.

The real estate agent who won my business and high school pep rallies share a critically important rainmaker attribute—a clearly defined goal. A pep rally on the Tuesday before a bye week would be hard-pressed to generate a modicum of excitement. In order to cheer with wild enthusiasm, we need to have a particular end in mind. We want to score the touchdown, block the kick, sack the quarterback, win the championship, and earn bragging rights. Generic cheers about doing one's best and trying hard would be annoyingly lame. (I do, however, have a soft spot in my heart for the somewhat generic cheer shouted by Harvard students when their team is losing: "That's all right. That's okay. You'll all work for us some day." It's a brilliant balloon-bursting sentiment that reminds one and all that football, basketball, and hockey are simply games, and the business of real life begins after the whistle blows.) Rainmaker marketing works the same way. It requires specificity and focus. Vague-sounding goals like "I'll work hard to get the best possible price" wither against a promise to "find new owners you'll be happy to entrust with your home." Emotion beats logic, and enthusiasm and passion feed emotional connections. Be true to your school and be true to the essence of rainmaking.

ROE #5

Say It Like You Mean It

I recently conducted a workshop with the rainmaking sales force of CLS Investments, a large third-party investment advisor. The workshop was focused on helping the wholesalers identify and build their personal brands. I began by asking them to define their business. Their responses revolved around the concept of "providing investment products to help individuals achieve financial security." They quickly realized how weak that sounded but were at a loss on how to proceed. So I asked them to name the business that Harley Davidson was in, and I gave them a hint that the answer was not manufacturing motorcycles. After some give-and-take, it was agreed that Harley is in the lifestyle business—most particularly a lifestyle that allows middle-aged accountants and attorneys to dress in black leather, roar down the road, scare the crap out of the common folk, and live out a James Dean fantasy (albeit before donning a suit and tie and heading back to the office).

That epiphany started a new wave of brainstorming and the crystallization of a marketing value proposition focused on the tangible benefits that CLS delivered to its clients. Unlike other wholesalers who were pitching somewhat commoditized products, CLS offered timesaving, turnkey solutions. By working with CLS, financial advisors could spend less time analyzing portfolios and more time prospecting and building relationships. The realization that they were in the time-management business prompted the CLS sales team to bill themselves as the "timesaving wholesalers"—thereby owning a position that is unique and distinct from the hundreds of other wholesalers that march through a financial advisor's office.

The lesson of this story is that if you don't know what business you're in (i.e., what people are buying rather than what you're selling), you won't know who can best benefit from your products and services. You won't know which prospects to target. You won't know how to better serve your existing clients. And most importantly, you won't know how to differentiate yourself and stand out from the competition.

One of the first and most important steps in creating a powerful personal brand is making a strong and memorable first impression. Suppose you're at a cocktail party and someone asks what you do for a living. Answering with a functional title like "I'm a financial advisor" or "I'm in sales" is a surefire conversation killer. Instead, position yourself in a way that focuses on the benefits you provide. For example, the financial advisor might say "I worry about my clients' money so they don't have to."

So what's your story? If you had to explain your business to a toddler or a septuagenarian, what would you say? Children and old people tend to get confused and frustrated with too many facts. (Actually people of all ages get frustrated with too many facts, but youngsters and oldsters are far more likely to make their frustration known.) The preferred approach is to share a story filled with analogies, metaphors, and examples. Years ago when my daughter, Julia, was very young she asked me what I did at work. For a moment my mind raced with intermingled concepts about customer segmentation, distribution channels, media plans, and the like. I quickly realized that she wouldn't have a clue what I was talking about so, instead, I reminded her of the commercial she had recently seen on television that made her want a Barbie Jeep. "That's kind of what Daddy does," I explained. "I make people want to buy the stuff that my company sells." I thought I had hit the nail on the head until she looked at me and said, "Does that mean you lie to people?"

"Why do you say that?" I asked.

"Because you said all the stuff on TV is garbage. That they make it look great but when you bring it home it's nothing but a piece of junk."

Clearly, this was a case where I would have been better off sticking to the facts and nothing but the facts—but my story did have its intended result and prompted my eight-year-old to gain a moderately accurate understanding of what I did during my prolonged absences from the house.

So, how would you—a rainmaker extraordinaire or wannabe—describe what you do in terms that a child could understand? And how would you phrase it in a way that prompts your audience to ask for more information? Consider these examples to jump-start the process:

- Real estate broker – "I'm a matchmaker between people and homes."

- Accountant – "I reduce taxes for business owners."

- Interior decorator – "I turn houses into homes."

- Management consultant – "I make one plus one equal three."

- Marketer – "I grease the skids for the sales team."

- Graphic artist – "I turn my clients' words into pictures."

- Attorney – "I protect clients from the enemies they don't even see."

Regardless of what business you're in, your clients and prospects are going to distill your message down to a single sentence. If you don't do it for them, they'll craft that one-sentence message themselves—taking it out of your control, which is not where a rainmaker ever wants to be.

The Elevator Speech

Most people refer to this single-sentence positioning statement as an "elevator speech." I prefer to view it as the opening salvo in a multilevel elevator encounter. It's designed to crisply articulate what you do, but it should never be viewed as an end unto itself. Like everything we do in marketing, this short positioning statement is intended to motivate the listener to request more information. And the last thing you want to do is stumble and mumble after eliciting a prospect's interest. So create a multifloor elevator speech that slowly builds upon itself—with each new level increasing the listener's desire and urgency to learn more.

Here's a sample I developed for I-Pension LLC, the innovative financial services firm that I co-founded with my longtime friend and colleague, Jane Mancini:

1st Floor   We provide professional money management for the people who need it most—middle-class Americans.

2nd Floor   Unlike most financial advisory firms who cater to clients with at least $250,000 or $500,000 of savings, we have no investment minimums.

3rd Floor   Despite having no minimum account size, we provide
             the same services that wealthy people receive—
             packaged in asset allocation models designed to fit
             every investment temperament and time horizon.

4th Floor   And we make it all very affordable—charging
             just $1 a day for 401(k) accounts (or $.50 a day for
             balances under $40,000) and 1% of assets for
             non-employer-sponsored accounts.

5th Floor   To top it off, we accomplish all this via personal
             attention with an investment advisor dedicated to
             your account and your needs. We're not a virtual
             company—we're a relationship company.

At this point, it's time to turn over the invisible microphone
to the listener by asking a simple open-ended question: "What
else can I tell you about how we help people?"

You've accomplished your goal—using a monologue to create
a dialogue.

ROE #6

Broaden Your Brandwidth

The term "branding" was first used in conjunction with the branding of cattle. Because cows and steer tend to look alike, branding was an effective way to identify them. Similarly, you probably look a lot like every other architect/consultant/ attorney/broker/whatever, and a unique brand would be an effective way to help stand out from the crowd.

The concept that individuals can actually have their own brand was introduced in 1997 when management guru, Tom Peters, wrote an article entitled "The Brand Called You," in *Fast Company* magazine. The article can be summarized in the following quote: "Regardless of age, regardless of position, regardless of the business we happen to be in, all of us need to understand the importance of branding. We are CEOs of our own companies: Me, Inc. To be in business today, our most important job is to be head marketer for the brand called 'You.'"

The essay was a huge hit and spawned countless imitators offering advice on how to build a powerful personal brand. Each of the rules of engagement introduced in this book plays an important role in building your personal brand, so rather than focusing on the whys and wherefores of personal branding, this chapter provides workbook-like exercises to help jump-start the process.

A SELF-ASSESSMENT

Asking questions is one of the best ways to learn about people, and it works equally well when the person you're questioning is yourself. Take some time to honestly answer these twenty questions.

1. What do you do for a living?

2. What part of your career do you most enjoy?

3. What part of your career do you most value?

4. What about you is unique?

5. How are you different from the competitor down the street?

6. What are you best known for?

7. How do you go above and beyond?

8. How would your clients describe you?

9. How would you like your clients to describe you?

10. Of the last three to five clients who chose to leave you and work with another firm, what were the primary drivers of their decision to leave?

11. Of the last three to five clients who chose to bring their business to you, what were the primary drivers of their decision to do so?

12. On your deathbed, what would you say to your children about what is important in life?

13. If one of your clients had to deliver a twenty-five-word eulogy about you, what would you want him or her to say?

14. Which of your clients would you like to clone?

15. Why would you like to clone that client?

16. In lieu of cloning, how can you locate additional clients like him or her?

17. What is the single biggest change you could make to grow your business?

18. What would your ideal day at the office look like?

19. What can you do to turn that ideal day into a day-to-day reality?

20. If you had the chance to begin your career all over again, what would you do differently?

ACTIVITY ASSESSMENT

This exercise will help you identify and rank the activities you do on behalf of your clients and in the day-to-day running of your business. It will provide a framework to assess which of those activities are most valuable, which could be decreased or eliminated without hurting your business, and which should be enhanced. And ideally, it will serve as a catalyst to identify new activities—ones that could help attract additional clients.

STEP ONE: List eight to twenty specific activities you do to run your business.

STEP TWO: Draw a grid like the one on page 33, and plot each of these activities in terms of how much time you dedicate to them and the relative value they provide to your clients and to growing your business.

STEP THREE: Now that you've identified the activities you undertake to run your business and have ranked them in terms of time and value, you can look toward the future. W. Chan Kim and Renee Mauborgne introduced "the eliminate-reduce-raise-create grid" in their insightful book, *Blue Ocean Strategy,* to do just that. Use the quadrants in the following grid to identify activities that could or should be eliminated, or that you should spend more or less time on. Use this opportunity to also consider adding activities not currently employed that could enhance your brand and further grow your business.

Eliminate	Increase
Reduce	Add

SWOT ANALYSIS

A key component of MBA programs and strategic planning initiatives, SWOT analyses provide an understandable framework to identify and assess your Strengths, Weaknesses, Opportunities, and Threats (both internal and external) as you grow your personal brand and your business. When used effectively, a SWOT analysis can provide a new and insightful perspective— one that can help separate you from the crowd.

Strengths	Weaknesses
Opportunities	Threats

As you complete your personal SWOT analysis, use the following questions to probe deeper and elicit the larger truths that often escape our scrutiny:

- Strengths – What personal and professional attributes are you most proud of? What about you do your competitors most fear? What resources and connections (people, experience, skills, etc.) can you employ? Why do clients sign on with you and stay with you? What is the most profitable area of your business? What type of business or client is a "slam dunk" for you to win?

- Weaknesses – What's the one thing you'd like to improve about yourself? Is there one particular negative about you that competitors point to when trying to gain an advantage? Are there issues or topics you try to avoid discussing with clients? Are there subject areas that you don't feel confident about? Are there resources you lack? Why do you lose clients or fail to convert prospects to clients? Is there an aspect of your business that consistently loses money?

- Opportunities – What marketplace, industry, or community trends can you leverage? How about demographics—does the aging of the huge baby boomer generation impact your business? Are there ways to better utilize technology? What competitor do you most admire and what can you learn from that firm or individual? Can your core competency be used to enter complementary market segments? Is there a niche market that competitors are ignoring?

- Threats – What keeps you up at night? What trends could weaken your position? What are colleagues or competitors doing that could diminish appeal for your services? Can your strengths be easily duplicated or leapfrogged? Is your product or service subject to commoditization or pricing pressures?

PUTTING IT TOGETHER

The highest achievers and most successful individuals in any field are those who view themselves as self-employed entrepreneurs—which is simply another definition of rainmaker. They run their own business within the framework of the larger business they're part of. Because of that, these individuals have a strong sense of their vision, value proposition, and mission. To truly succeed as a rainmaking marketer, you need to follow their example.

Several of the rules of engagement specifically address the need for a clearly articulated statement of who you are, what you do, and how you benefit your clients. (In particular see ROE #5: Say It Like You Mean It; ROE #8: Stay Up, Sell Out, Cash In; and ROE #12: Manifest Your Destiny.) In addition to *Marketing for Rainmakers*, there are a variety of other resources to help you tackle the admittedly difficult task of distilling your values, experience, and expertise into a concise and readily understood statement. Here's a sampling of web sites featuring free assistance and interactive tools to help in developing your personalized mission statements and value propositions:

- http://www.franklincovey.com/fc/library_and_resources/ mission_statement_builder

- http://nightingale.com/mission_select.aspx

- http://www.quintcareers.com/creating_personal_mission_ statements.html

- http://www.time-management-tips-and-skills.com/ personal-mission-statement.html

Rather than typing in these URLs, you can visit my web site—www.MarketingForRainmakers.com—and use the hyperlinks to direct your browser to these tools.

You should also visit the web site to download the free "Marketing for Rainmakers Personal Branding Workbook."

ROE #7

Bow to the Wow

Marketing is like sex. Not male sex, mind you, but rather female sex. To the male of the species when sex is good, it's great; and when sex is bad, it's still good. To the more self-actualized half of our species, however, good sex is indeed great, but bad sex is somewhere on the spectrum between doing laundry and having a root canal.

Similarly, good marketing elicits wows, while bad—or even mediocre—marketing induces yawns. And because we're talking about marketing for rainmakers, wow is the only goal we should be aiming for. As management guru Tom Peters explains it, "Being average has never had much appeal. Better to fail with flair in pursuit of something neat." (My only quibble with Mr. Peters is his use of the word "neat." It doesn't sound particularly aspirational.)

Let's start by defining "wow." At its simplest it means delivering a product or experience that truly delights and exceeds customer expectations. It's a little more complicated than that, however, because there are actually two varieties of wow experiences. There's the intellectual wow and the emotional, heartfelt wow. The former is more aptly thought of as a "cool" rather than a true wow. And because this chapter is entitled "Bow to the Wow" rather than "Drool for the Cool," you can safely assume that emotional, heartfelt wows are what we should be aiming for. Cool wows are ephemeral while heartfelt wows are forever.

Think about the first time you heard about TiVo and its ability to pause live-action television, provide your own version of instant replays, and help identify programs that might be of interest. That was a cool wow. The first convertible with a folding hardtop was also a cool wow, as were GPS navigation systems, camera phones, and HD television. What's truly interesting, however, is that all of these cool-wow epiphanies quickly became mainstays of our daily lives. With the exception of the convertible, all are available at Wal-Mart, Target, and Amazon. What was once a cool wow is now a ho-hum.

The staying power of cool wow is quite limited for new ideas and inventions. If it's a good idea, it will be copied. You'll still enjoy the first-mover advantage, but the wows you elicit will be fewer and further between. The single best way to get to the Platonic ideal of wow and stay there is by creating and delivering an outstanding overall customer experience that can only be duplicated by cloning people's attitudes and passion. (Of course, the company that accomplishes that will have achieved a wow second only to the invention of the wheel.)

Here's a personal example of a heartfelt wow. I recently had to ship a laptop back to the manufacturer for a repair and was instructed to use DHL. I called DHL's 800-number and scheduled a home pick-up via an exceptionally fast and friendly automated interface. I never had to provide a name or number.

The automated system captured my address from the telephone I called from, and the DHL truck appeared within the hour. Prior to this experience, all my shipping had been done via FedEx or UPS. I would never have thought of using DHL. But now I will.

The more persnickety of you might argue that this type of experience is driven by innovative technology and thus falls into the "cool" category of wow. The difference, however, is that the technology used by DHL is not particularly new or innovative. The wow is generated by the way the technology anticipates and delivers an emotionally satisfying customer experience.

Another recent wow experience occurred when I walked into the local Zoots dry cleaning store and the clerk had my clean laundry waiting for me as I approached the counter. I actually blurted out an audible "Wow!" and asked the clerk how he had done that. He smiled and said he had seen me pull my car into the parking lot, typed my name into the system, and retrieved my shirts. He said remembering people's names and surprising them made the job more fun. It also makes me keep going back.

As job responsibilities go, rainmakers have multiple opportunities to deliver heartfelt-wow experiences because the very nature of their jobs brings them close to the end-user. The client is known and a personal relationship exists. The interesting thing about personal relationships is that the "little things" truly are most important and most meaningful. Assuming that my relationship with my wife is similar to most spousal relationships, I can elicit a far stronger and more sincere heartfelt wow from her by doing laundry (without being asked), emptying the dishwasher (without being asked), and picking up the family room (without being asked) than any amount of baubles and bling could ever elicit. It's the same way with your clients. The effort you spend on the little things like common courtesy, personalized service, and frequent communications will pay huge dividends in customer loyalty, satisfaction, and retention. And it ain't rocket science; rather it's things like:

- Handwritten notes – Mont Blanc sells a lot of high-end pens to rainmakers, and the best way to put them to use is via handwritten notes to clients. In this age of email and instant messaging, nothing stands out like a handwritten note of thanks.

- Follow-up calls – Rainmakers solve problems and deliver solutions, but it's very easy to close one case file and move on to the next without looking back. Calling a client a few weeks or months after a project is completed to check on how everything worked out will elicit louder wows than most anything else you can do. It shows you still care even when your time is not billable.

- Client feedback – "Post-mortem" reviews are standard practice for large-scale IT projects. These roundtable discussions consider the completed project from all perspectives— including the end user's. Professional service providers can gain valuable insight by asking clients simple questions like "Were your expectations met?" "What disappointed you?" "What could I have done better?" "Were there any surprises?" Your clients will appreciate your interest, and you'll move up a couple of rungs in the client's eye compared to other service providers who don't bother to ask. This also works for proposals you lost to a competitor. Probe to find out why you lost out. You still won't get the business, but you'll have a much better shot next time around.

- Expense control – Rainmaker professional service providers charge a lot of money for their expertise; and because they're successful, they don't need to gouge every last penny from their clients. It's counterintuitive, but educating clients on how to control expenses will likely result in generating more billable hours rather than fewer. I recently worked with Brown Rudnick, a large Boston law firm, and I was very impressed when one of the partners explained that he wouldn't participate on a particular conference call because there was no reason for me to pay his hourly fee when a junior associate could very capably handle the matter at hand. That's a wow by any definition.

- Fore and aft communication – One of the most common techniques when giving presentations is to "tell'em what you're going to tell'em, tell'em, and then tell'em what you told'em." For rainmakers, this approach translates to ongoing, comprehensive communications with your client. At the beginning, you can create a heartfelt wow just by sending along a list of questions the client should be prepared to answer at your kickoff meeting. You can also supplement your standard, legalese engagement contract with a conversational explanation of what charges will likely be incurred, how they'll be billed, etc. An information sheet with the names, telephone numbers, and email addresses of all the people the client will interact with can also increase client satisfaction. During the project, return client calls quickly, don't keep clients waiting on the phone or in your reception area, and keep your eyes open to the nuances of behavior or speech that could signal client dissatisfaction with some element of the project. At the end of the project, in addition to the postmortem and mandatory, handwritten thank-you note described above, meet with the client to review the aggregated charges and highlight the value delivered.

The point of all this is that most of what rainmakers, salespeople, and marketers do on a daily basis is simply part of conducting business on a level playing field. The really important stuff, however, is getting your customers to say "Wow! These guys really:"

- "Get it."

- "Understand my needs."

- "Know what they're doing."

- "Are looking down the road."

- "See the big picture."

- "Make my life easier, more fun, and more rewarding."

The best marketers and the most successful rainmakers bow at the altar of *Wow* to venerate their clients and engender a similar level of respect.

ROE #8

Stay Up, Sell Out, Cash In

There were two things I learned when my daughter was a baby. The first is that nothing can possibly prepare you for the miracle of birth and the feeling of all-consuming joy that comes from nuzzling your newborn's cheek and hearing her gurgle with delight. The second is that today's best marketing occurs between the hours of midnight and four o'clock in the morning—the prime time of infomercials.

To a lot of people, infomercials exemplify everything that's wrong with modern society. They're crass, materialistic, demeaning, and manipulative. On the flip side, however, they're also passionate, interactive, and fanatically single-minded. Best of all, they're jam-packed with reasons to buy and they exude a palpable sense of urgency to buy *now*. In many respects, they represent the Platonic ideal of *Marketing for Rainmakers*.

If I ruled the world—as perhaps I should—every business would be required to create an infomercial about their products or services. Sophisticated marketers would have to swallow their pride and go slumming down the back alleys where their more primitive brethren practice their seedy craft. And what would be the point of such an exercise? Simply that it would crystallize your story. It would force you to imbue life and energy into your brand's value proposition, your unique selling proposition, and all the other BS propositions that marketers spend far too much time developing and hiding behind.

It would also force professional marketers to hold themselves accountable for results because, of all the activities marketers are involved in, infomercials are the easiest to measure. They either work or they don't work. People call the 1-800 number or visit the web site. And they either do it on the spot, or they don't do it at all. There's no hiding behind the traditional marketing whine that "50 percent of all advertising dollars are wasted, I just don't know which 50 percent." The ROI of infomercials is either positive or negative, and that buck-nakedness for all to see is one scary proposition for the vast majority of professional marketers.

The act of writing and storyboarding an infomercial will require a fresh look at everything you do to promote your products and services. It will force you to put yourself in the place of your customers, develop a well rehearsed and carefully choreographed elevator pitch, and focus solely on what your customers will see and hear (and most importantly, what they *feel* about what they see and hear).

Here's how to do it:

- Identify the make-up of your audiences—both the in-studio audience who will gasp and applaud on cue, and the at-home audience who'll be watching on television while munching snacks and being distracted by kids, chores, pets, insomnia, and all the other headaches of day-to-day life. This step of identifying your audience is critical because it will drive every other aspect of your infomercial.

- Determine the format for the infomercial. Will it look and feel like a talk show, a small group discussion, or a lecture? Will it feature a product demonstration, testimonials, and/or hands-on training? Will it be informative, entertaining, or sentimental?

- Select your spokesperson. Should it be a man or a woman? Young or old? Should she be dressed casually or formally? Street clothes or specialized dress (e.g., like a scientist, a healthcare provider, or a nerdy academic)? Should she speak with a down-home twang, an aristocratic air, or a pedantic drone?

- Zero in on the number one benefit that your product or service provides. (This is your hook, so choose it carefully.) Then identify half a dozen corollary benefits that build off of or tie into this primary benefit.

- Determine your selling price. Make sure it's neither too high nor too low—and above all, make certain it appears to provide exceptional value. (The natural tendency here is to simply use your company's existing pricing structure. As part of this exercise, however, I'd encourage you to start from scratch, revisit all your old assumptions, and accept the fact that price is a key part of every sales/marketing equation.)

- Articulate why the purchase decision needs to be made today, on the spot, while the 1-800 number is being displayed on the screen. It doesn't matter if you're selling a complex multiplatform enterprise-wide system that normally requires a six-month RFP process and a papal blessing. Make believe the decision can be made today—and then state why it *should* be made today.

- Identify an act-now incentive that will appeal to the fence-sitters in your audience. Assuming that a set of steak knives won't pass muster, how about a free consultation, a 10 percent discount, onsite training, an extended warranty, dedicated telephone support, below-rate financing, or free installation. The key thing is to be creative, understand what would motivate your audience, and then package it in an irresistible offer that even the Godfather couldn't refuse.

When you're done outlining your infomercial, you'll have created a roadmap for all your subsequent marketing efforts. What may have felt like a sellout at first will, in the end, help you sell out your products and services.

Infomercials and AIDA

Infomercials follow the classic AIDA model that has ruled the direct marketing world for almost a century. AIDA stands for Attention, Interest, Desire, and Action; and while it is ridiculously simplistic and manipulative, it does provide a useful checklist for building and delivering a compelling sales script and it can be used as a guide for all your marketing efforts. The AIDA model works like this:

- Attention – We live in a world of information and sensory overload. In order to grab someone's attention, you need to divert it from something else. If you don't engage the audience during the first few moments of your interaction, then your first impression will be your last.

- Interest – Once you've gained someone's attention—typically via a monologue—your communication needs to evolve naturally into a dialogue that's focused on the customer's needs. Forget about what's important to you, because that's of interest only to you.

- Desire – The next stage in the selling process is to engender desire. Most marketers and sales people skip or gloss over this step. They confuse need with desire. The customer may recognize his need for what you're offering but, for any one of a thousand reasons, not feel compelled to satisfy it. Desire is the emotional manifestation of a need, and it's best generated via visualization of what life would be like after satisfying the need (e.g., via testimonials, before-and-after scenarios, and other storytelling techniques). Once you create desire, the next step is a cinch.

- Action – This step closes the deal. It has to be straightforward and simple: "Do this and get that." Anything more and you risk losing all the goodwill you've created.

Section Two

The Strategic
Rainmaking Marketer

ROE #9

SEE THE FOREST IN EVERY TREE

There's an apocryphal story that goes like this. A man is walking down the street when he comes across three men laying bricks. He pauses to watch them and then walks over to the first man. "What are you doing?" he asks. The first bricklayer shrugs and, without even looking up, says, "I'm making $15 an hour." The man then moves on to the second bricklayer and asks the same question, "What are you doing?" The second bricklayer glances up and says, "I'm building a wall." The man walks over to the third bricklayer and again asks the same question, "What are you doing?" The third bricklayer stands straight up and proudly points to the heavens. "I'm building a cathedral," he proclaims.

Wow. What a different approach to work. Indeed, what a different approach to life. And, most relevantly, what a different approach to sales, marketing, and rainmaking.

Ask yourself and your colleagues that same question— "What are you doing?"—several times a day. If the response is "preparing a pitch book," "building a mailing list," or "doing a socio-economic overlay on our top 1000 customers," then you're focusing on the task rather than the vision. And while it's vitally important to do every task well—because that will ensure the quality of the final product—the task cannot become an end onto itself. Tasks are the means to an end. They are the building blocks of cathedrals—and the seeds of rainmaking.

So what's an ROE-inspired response to the question of "What are you doing?" Well it would be more along the lines of "contributing to our goal of increasing sales by 50 percent." Or "reminding our clients why they selected us in the first place." Or "building an entrepreneurial corporate culture." Or maybe even "putting one more nail in our competitor's coffin."

What's the difference? One focuses on the big picture and one on the small. One sees the forest and one sees the trees. Successful rainmakers meld both approaches and have the ability to see the forest in every tree. It's a rare attribute but one that's well worth cultivating—and one that will provide a rich harvest for many years to come.

The "Too Smart for Their Own Good" Corollary

This problem of not seeing the forest for the trees has special significance for professional service providers like attorneys, accountants, architects, and other highly credentialed specialists. In their case, they often allow overreliance on their technical expertise to interfere with the development of a thought-leader mindset. We've all heard stories about the brilliant medical doctor with the horrible bedside manner. What we hear less about, but which is equally common, are professionals who believe that all they need to do is study hard, decide on a specialty, do consistently fine work, and the world will beat a path to their door. Then they become irritable and confused when that doesn't happen.

Expertise in almost every field is rapidly becoming a commodity. MBAs and other graduate degrees are the equivalent of what an undergraduate degree was just one generation ago. In addition to the danger of becoming a society of overeducated robo-technocrats, we're well into the process of confusing book-learning with true insight and wisdom. Memorizing the multiplication tables does not a mathematician make. Nor does the ability to cite chapter and verse of the Federal tax code demonstrate that an attorney can effectively contribute to building an estate plan involving dueling siblings, a widowed trophy wife, a handicapped child, a charitable trust, two accountants, and a host of financial advisors. Knowledge does not automatically translate into wisdom. The facts don't extrapolate themselves into insight. And epiphanies don't happen just because you connect the visible dots. You also need to see the invisible dots and make the connections that have eluded everyone else.

Think about it as the difference between the workings of the conscious and subconscious minds. Learning and knowledge occur at the conscious level and, almost by definition, only scratch the surface of true understanding. This is the layer where data gathering and analysis occur. It's the level playing field that every professional service provider operates on. It's a place where reputations can be lost—due to inadequate training, sloppiness, or oversight—but it is not where reputations are made.

The true measure of one's professional abilities—and rainmaking skills—occurs at the deeper subconscious level. This is where the complex process of internalization, integration, and synthesis occurs. This is where facts become truths, and observation is replaced by true understanding. This is where the heart of rainmaking resides.

It can also be a scary place for professionals. Harry Truman once defined an expert as "a person who is afraid to learn

anything new because then he wouldn't be an expert anymore."
What was true in Harry's day is still true today. Our expertise
makes us comfortable. It's a professional security blanket. It
provides an element of status, self-worth, and self-confidence—all
of which are great attributes. However, today's clients are looking
for more than technical expertise. They want true business
partners and advisors. They're looking for collaborators who can
work across functional or departmental boundaries.

In short, your clients and prospects have plenty of "dots"—
and they can probably connect most or all of them. What they
need, however, is someone who can read the spaces in between
and reveal the hidden picture.

TIPS ON BECOMING A BIG-PICTURE, INVISIBLE-DOT CONNECTOR

- Goof off – Medical research has demonstrated that our brains
  function better with rest. Much of the extrapolation and
  synthesis happens behind the scenes. While our bodies are
  focused on lining up a golf putt, shampooing our hair, or
  watching *American Idol*, our brains are feverishly at work
  sorting data points, conducting regression analyses, and
  otherwise synthesizing facts, nuances, and inferences into a
  coherent "a-ha" realization.

- Get over yourself – Much of the reason sales and marketing
  rainmaker-types fail to see the big picture is that their own
  egos get in the way. Forget about trying to prove how smart
  you are and, instead, demonstrate how valuable you are.

- Risk it – Breakthrough thinking rarely happens when bounded
  by constraints. And while risk management is generally a good

thing, risk avoidance can close your eyes to the possibilities that can lead to breakthrough insights.

- Be devilish – Creative thinking requires a devil's advocate approach to business. Ask yourself the tough questions, so you can provide easy answers to your clients. (See ROE #15: Muddy the Waters, for more insight on the benefits of being a devil's advocate.)

- Turn it upside down – When young artists are learning their craft, their teachers will often tell them to turn the item or image that they are painting or drawing upside down. Doing so tricks the brain into not trying to precisely replicate the particular portrait or still life. Instead, the brain focuses on the interplay of lines and shadows and strives to recreate them with every stroke. Without the intimidating constraint of trying to *match* a Degas or Vermeer, the artists are free to go wherever their eyes, fingers, and souls lead them. Similarly, as you try to make sense of a particular issue or project, consider how it would look upside down, through a prism, or reflected in a mirror. You'll be able to see the spaces as well as the spaces in between.

ROE #10

FEED THE LION AND SPARE THE MOUSE

I have very fond memories of enjoying a summer afternoon at my cousin's house in Maryland, sitting outside on the deck, drinking beer, and enjoying a bucket of steamed crabs heavily sprinkled with Old Bay seasoning. In addition to the great company and spirited conversation, I distinctly remember thinking that there was a perfect balance about the moment. The beer was replenishing the perspiration that dripped into the heavy air, and the crabs required just as much effort to crack open and eat as they provided in caloric intake. I figured I could eat as much as I wanted and never gain an ounce, and I wondered why no one had ever engineered a diet craze based on eating nothing but steamed crabs. I quickly realized, however, that subsisting on steamed crabs was an impossibility and I would eventually starve to death.

Lions face a similar conundrum. While it would be very easy for a lion to hunt and kill a mouse, it would starve to death in the process. The amount of energy expended to capture and eat a mouse exceeds the amount of calories ingested. So while mouse-hunting would provide some immediate gratification to the lion, in the long run it would prove deadly. Which is why lions hunt big game like zebras and antelopes. The same concept applies to rainmaking marketers—focusing on small wins to the exclusion of large wins could spell disaster. The flip side for both lions and rainmakers is that they would also starve to death if they solely hunted elephants.

So how do you distinguish between mice, zebras, and elephants in the business world? And just as importantly, how do you avoid the armadillos, porcupines, and tortoises that are easy to catch but painful to swallow? You do it by comparing your current meal plan to the Rainmaker's Food Pyramid and faithfully adhering to these basic nutritional principles:

- Hunt to kill – Time is your most valuable commodity, but it's easy to waste time on prospects that look attractive and always seem on the verge of making a decision but, in the end, never become paying clients. When confronted with these noncommittal critters, you're better off taking your best shot, affirming that you are available to provide more information, but setting your sights elsewhere.

- Be a sharpshooter – While a shotgun approach does provide a greater chance of hitting *something*, selective hunting with a rifle will deliver higher quality clientele, superior conversion rates, and increased retention. As you do indeed eat what you kill, rifle shooting will better ensure that your meal is well balanced, satisfying, and of your own choosing.

- Take small bites and eat slowly – Unless you're the youngest in a family of ten, mealtime should be a civilized experience rather than a frenetic grub grab. Similarly, taking on too many clients too quickly in an attempt to build a business can actually destroy the business. The motherly rejoinder that "your eyes are bigger than your stomach" is equally relevant to business. It's easy to get caught up in the moment and welcome any business that comes your way. The downside to business gluttony is the increased likelihood of compromising the quality and timeliness of your work because you're spread too thin, thereby disenchanting new and old customers alike. Don't allow fear of starvation to cause death by indigestion.

- Savor every morsel – While you and your colleagues will recognize and appreciate the differences between your mouse-like and antelope-like clients, never allow your clients to sense the difference. In the business world, mice aspire to be antelopes, and antelopes aspire to be elephants. They all make a contribution to your company's success and should be treated accordingly. The truth of this principle became all too clear to me during a conversation with an account executive at a web development firm I had hired. Our relatively simple request to modify some existing functionality was taking forever to complete and I called our account exec to see how we could speed up the process. As part of his explanation for the delay, the account exec told me they were working with over three hundred clients. Because the account exec was young and trying to do a good job, and because he clearly had not been trained very well, I refrained from exploding at the lunacy of such a comment. Instead, using my most avuncular tone, I explained that I as a customer didn't care about that. As far as I was concerned, I was the only customer he had and probably his favorite as well. I told him to never repeat that statement with another client because it was equivalent to telling someone that he was merely a number rather than a sentient being. After my well-restrained lecture, he agreed to think before he spoke and to remedy our problem, which he did.

- Pass the sniff test – Even my yellow Labrador Retriever, Ruby, whose only apparent goal in life is to eat as much as possible, will not eat something without smelling it first. And she will indeed walk away from morsels that look delectable but don't pass her personal sniff test. I don't claim to understand Ruby's sniff criteria, but I know she has some—and you should as well. If a client or prospect doesn't feel right, he or she probably isn't right. You have the ability to say no and walk away if your gut tells you to. It isn't personal, it's business— and at the beginning and end of the day, it's your business.

THE RAINMAKER'S FOOD PYRAMID

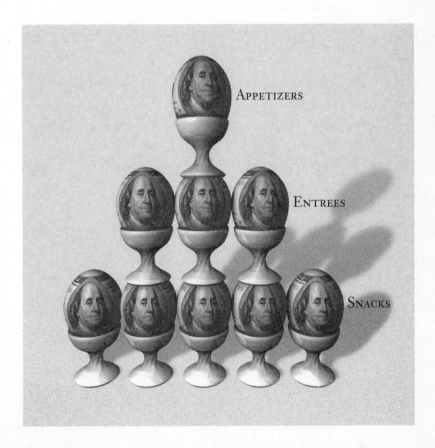

Appetizers

This is where you can taste-test the waters and expand beyond your core market. View this client segment as an opportunity to pilot products, services, and programs to drive future growth. Pro bono and community service work would also fall in this category.

Entrees

This is your area of expertise and niche domination. The majority of your time and energy should be spent on this segment of the market—defending your turf, attracting add-on business from existing clients, and winning referrals.

Snacks

These are the transactional clients whose business is often mundane and short-lived, but who help pay the bills. Sometimes, you take on these clients as a "favor" to important clients. For example, a financial advisor with a million-dollar minimum account size will often accept smaller accounts for the children or siblings of an affluent client.

ROE #11

SMARTEN UP

Remember the good old days when clients accepted a professional's advice and recommendations without ever asking a question or voicing a concern? It's quite different today. People have been conditioned to question virtually every decision they make in every aspect of their lives—up to and including their investment portfolios, tax strategies, interior design color palettes, legal matters, architectural detail, and medical diagnoses and treatments. So, just as they relied upon *Consumer Reports* to guide their appliance and automobile purchases in the past, today's individuals and corporate businesspeople are apt to utilize Google searches, online calculators, talk radio, chat rooms, WebMD, blogs, vlogs, and Epinions-like social networking web sites to help them make an informed decision.

Unfortunately, a little knowledge remains a dangerous thing—a fact which is exacerbated by human beings' tendency to overestimate their knowledge of just about everything from the yield curve to the optimal R-factor of insulated glass. There's even a name for this tendency to believe one possesses intelligence and capabilities that far exceed the average: the Lake Wobegon effect. This narcissistic tendency is named for the idyllic town made famous on Garrison Keillor's *Prairie Home Companion* radio series—a town where "all the women are strong, all the men are good-looking, and all the children are above average." Considerable research has been done on the Lake Wobegon effect, including a classic Swedish study in which 80 percent of respondents rated themselves among the top 30 percent of all drivers. Similarly, a College Board survey asked high school seniors to rate themselves in their ability to "get along with others." Sixty percent of students rated themselves in the top ten percent, and a truly astounding quarter of them rated themselves in the top one percent. Perhaps most telling is that less than one percent rated themselves below average.

All of this translates into opportunity for savvy and responsive marketers. Prospects and customers want to become knowledgeable and have access to all relevant information before making purchase decisions. The opportunity is to provide this information yourself, thereby lessening their need to look elsewhere and further strengthening your position as their go-to expert. This opportunity can best be addressed via "knowledge-added" marketing—as opposed to the more widespread but less effective "value-added" school of marketing. Value-added marketing has been all the rage since the 1980s. It introduced the concept of focusing on building relationships, understanding clients and their needs, and then providing insightful and creative ways to satisfy those needs. It replaced the "make them buy what you're selling" paradigm with a kinder, gentler "sell them what they want and need" mantra. The flipside of the value-added approach, however, is that value-added was often reduced to simply throwing more features at the client to see what stuck. And because value is ultimately defined and measured by your clients, what you believe to be value-added services may indeed be embraced by some but will likely be rejected by scores of others.

Knowledge-added marketing puts the ball back in your court. Knowledge—defined as the effective dissemination of useful and pertinent information—is more of an absolute. It's quantitative rather than qualitative. If clients choose to ignore the information and knowledge you share, they do so at their own peril; and you can rest comfortably knowing you've done the right thing.

Knowledge-added marketing also addresses the biggest concern of every industry, profession, and marketer—having their product or service become a commodity. The focus of good marketing is identifying the one thing in your business that can never be commoditized. And 99 times out of 100, that one thing will be *knowledge*. Strive to get yourself into the knowledge business—whatever your business—and you'll become an invaluable resource and partner to your customers and distribution partners.

As you enter the knowledge business it's important to recognize that imparting knowledge is quite different from giving advice. The latter is more of a monologue, while the former requires a give-and-take dialogue. Giving advice is dictation, while sharing knowledge is collaboration. This distinction is especially important to rainmaking professional service providers whose stock-in-trade has long been the proffering of advice. You'll still provide advice and counsel, but it will be preceded with client-focused education.

In its purest form, knowledge-added marketing creates shared ownership of the product-research and competitive comparison process. There is a clear teacher-student hierarchy, but there is also a greater appreciation on the part of the student for the knowledge, skill set, and insight of the teacher. It's akin to the proverb about teaching a man to fish rather than giving him a fish. In the case of knowledge-added marketing, the adage would state, "if you teach a man to fish—he'll better appreciate a master fisherman."

Knowledge-added marketing requires a totally different approach to how you view and manage your business. Top-performing rainmakers never sell a thing. Instead, they provide all the information a client needs to make an intelligent and defensible decision and, in the process, they create an environment in which a purchase is the only logical conclusion. This education process also serves to help clients better understand the value you and your firm bring to the table. The client's understanding of your accretive role then helps build a loyalty-inspired barrier against competitive inroads, creating a customer base that is far less likely to stray when it comes time to make the next purchase.

The most common objection to knowledge-added marketing is that it lengthens the sales process. In reality, the opposite is true. Knowledge-added marketing greatly accelerates the client's learning curve because it addresses common issues and concerns upfront via non-product-specific materials and tools. It creates a more collaborative *quid pro quo* relationship in which the client learns about us and we learn about them. An additional benefit accrues, as a type of osmosis, during the process of creating educational materials. Education works best in bite-size pieces, so as we pare down our vast amount of knowledge into digestible "lessons" we start seeing things from a different perspective—the customer's. We consider what information is relevant and what is extraneous. We fine-tune our positioning and our story in a way that makes them far more powerful and memorable. We end up with a lesson plan that teaches our customers and ourselves why we are indeed the standard against which all others are measured.

The second most common objection to knowledge-added marketing is the concern about "giving away the farm." Can we educate clients to the point where they no longer need us and can instead do it themselves? Not likely. The underpinnings of knowledge-added marketing are a mutual respect for each party's respective expertise and specialty. In reality, the more clients understand what we do and how we do it, the more they recognize and appreciate the value we deliver. They don't want to do your job any more than you want to do theirs. Their goal is to focus on what they do best and allow folks like you to do the rest. It's a mutually beneficial relationship built on a strong foundation of trust, credibility, and learning.

SMART MOVES

Here are some simple ways to incorporate knowledge-added marketing into your business.

- Provide context – Learning comes faster and is better retained when delivered within the "student's" frame of reference. Don't simply provide a litany of facts; instead wrap them in a case study or a human-interest story that demonstrates how the information could benefit the reader.

- Think broadly – Integrate knowledge-added marketing into all of your promotional efforts rather than viewing it as a separate "educational" program. White papers and research reports are great starting points, but don't ignore corporate brochures, flyers, newsletters, web sites, blogs, podcasts, tip sheets, seminars, bylined articles, media interviews, and every other means you have to communicate with clients. Think of yourself as a teaching rainmaker and don't ever miss an opportunity to share and educate.

- Forget what you're selling – The less you mention your product name, the more attention you'll command. Your job as an educator is getting the customer to recognize that there's a problem and a solution. Emphasizing your specific product from the get-go makes the prospect focus on what's in it for you; emphasizing the larger need makes the prospect focus on what's in it for himself.

- Don't educate beyond the close – Like every other aspect of sales and marketing, you need to closely read your audience. You have to recognize information overload long before it arrives. Knowledge-added marketing does not try to make someone an expert. Rather, it is a way of conducting business that enhances credibility, builds rapport, and inspires confidence. As a rainmaker, what you've done is create the ideal environment to close the deal. And while education should certainly continue after the sale is made, closing the deal is the ultimate knowledge-added bottom line.

ROE #12

Manifest Your Destiny

Most sales and marketing programs are doomed from the start because they are not conceived and implemented as part of a grand vision. The vast majority are one-offs that are totally tactical in nature. They are not viewed as elements in a master plan; and they don't succeed in moving the company forward—largely because there is no clear pathway that leads forward. There is no direction, no focus, and no end in sight.

When companies or individuals realize this predicament, their first impulse is to write a mission statement, supported by a unique selling proposition (USP) and supplemented with a litany of syrupy corporate values. The mission statement gets posted on the corporate intranet site, the USP is introduced at a company-wide meeting or conference call, and the values are printed on posters, framed, and proudly displayed in conference rooms and hallways. At this point, they are quickly forgotten and ignored and the corporate meandering begins again.

In the *Marketing for Rainmakers* approach to business, it is critical to put pen to paper to identify your vision and chart your course. The simple act of writing is one of the most powerful catalysts for breakthrough thinking. Putting ideas on paper—out there for everyone to see and critique—helps ensure the clarity and consistency of your message, your goal, and your direction. Even when working alone, the process of writing serves to generate new ideas. Writing helps to test concepts and, through the self-editing process, consider alternatives and enhancements. In his book, *Lincoln's Sword*, Douglas Wilson explains that writing constituted a form of refuge for Abraham Lincoln, "a place of intellectual retreat from the chaos and confusion of office where he could sort through conflicting options and order his thoughts with words."

Words by themselves, however, can only get you so far. To truly be effective, your vision and strategy—as was the case with President Lincoln—need to be backed with passion and commitment. They also need to be meaningful and credible. Most employees laugh or cringe when they read their companies' value proposition. The words on the framed posters seem grossly disconnected to the company they work for. The statements tend to be self-serving, generic, and hardly inspirational.

Companies spend hundreds of hours of executive's time at offsite strategic retreats crafting mission and vision statements. Oftentimes, they also incur huge expenses by bringing in highly paid facilitators to help guide the discussion and drive consensus. But it's usually all for naught. Think about your own business for a moment. Can you articulate your corporate mission statement or value proposition? Even more tellingly, can you state the mission or USP of any of the hundreds of companies whose products and services you use? And do you care?

Mission statements to most companies are just another thing to check off the list. They're a necessary evil. No one enjoys writing them and no one enjoys reading them, which is why they enter a black hole once completed. So let's agree right here to never again entertain the creation of a mission statement and, instead, focus our efforts on creating a *manifesto*.

A manifesto is typically defined as a public declaration of one's principles, policies, intentions, opinions, objectives, and motives. It is usually associated with politics and is often used to incite action and insurgency. The most famous manifesto is the "Declaration of Independence" and, unlike any corporate mission statement before or since, it has gracefully withstood the passing of time.

For our purposes, let's define a manifesto as an unequivocal and impassioned statement of who you are and how you're going to change the world (or, at least, make the world a better place for your clients). Rather than an impersonal and vague mission statement that collects dust, a manifesto will serve as the springboard and litmus test for every aspect of your strategic plan. Look back at the definition of manifesto. It includes intentions, objectives, and motives—in other words it tells the world what the authoring body is going to do, why they're doing it, and how they're going to do it. It describes exactly what success would look like—so progress can be measured and monitored.

Most political manifestos are long, rambling, self-indulgent treatises. A rainmaker manifesto, on the other hand, is brief and pointed. It serves the dual purpose of expressing your strategy and serving as a rallying cry for success. Phil Knight powerfully expressed Nike's manifesto in just two words: *Crush Adidas*. With that visceral image drilled into their psyches, it's inconceivable that any of Nike's employees—from product designers to sales representatives—would be confused over priorities or objectives. Sam Walton crafted a manifesto for Wal-Mart, *To give ordinary folk the chance to buy the same thing as rich people*, that ensured total alignment within every department in the company. Disney also has a powerfully simple corporate manifesto, *To make people happy*, that is supported by specific examples of expected behaviors including the nurturing of wholesome American values, a fanatical attention to detail, and maintaining a culture of creativity and imagination.

The most powerful manifestos are grand in scale, akin to President Kennedy's bold statement that "We will put a man on the moon by the end of the decade." On the corporate front, an aspirational manifesto was put forth by Henry Ford in the early 1900s when he stated that "Ford will democratize the automobile." A similarly bold manifesto guided Sony in the 1950s to "Become the company most known for changing the worldwide poor-quality image of Japanese products."

As a rainmaker, you have the opportunity to create a uniquely powerful manifesto to keep both eyes focused on the prize. One of the best financial wholesalers I worked with liked to share his personal manifesto with every broker and advisor he worked with. Early on at introductory meetings he would say, "I'm looking to work with one hundred advisors who can each write one million dollars of business a year, and then I'll service the hell out of them." This statement painted a very clear picture of the mutually beneficial relationship he could deliver. And it worked because everyone likes to be part of a select group—especially when expectations and benefits are clearly articulated upfront.

Your own manifesto must reflect your personal style, beliefs, and ambitions. It should be a reach but still be achievable within a given timeframe. And, unlike the corporate-speak mission statements that camouflage rather than clarify, your personal manifesto will not need to be printed and framed. It will represent a crystallization of who you are and what you do—and will never be forgotten.

MANIFEST YOUR WORKDAY

Your personal manifesto presents a big-picture, strategic game plan for long-term success. Equally important, however, is the day-to-day execution of tactical projects and initiatives. This is where the proverbial best-laid plans tend to go awry—with the most frequent cause being a failure to apply the appropriate level of attention to preparing for client interactions. Sales-oriented rainmaker-wannabes are the biggest offenders in this regard. They have the mistaken belief that one's expertise and experience negate the need to prepare for sales calls or client meetings. As a result, they'll walk into a meeting and "wing it" without having written, researched, and *rehearsed* their presentation. Too often, in fact, they will approach a client meeting without identifying the goal of the meeting, the type and sequence of probing questions to ask, the likely objections or concerns the client might voice or, most importantly, the close. Sales presentations that are approached in this manner, without preplanning, are almost always doomed to failure.

The great football strategist, Vince Lombardi, was fond of saying "Plan your work, and work your plan." And like all football coaches, he maintained a comprehensive playbook that he and his assistants continually updated. Similarly, the most effective rainmakers develop their own sales and marketing playbook to help guide their day-to-day interactions with clients and prospects. The playbook is a living document that is continually edited and refined based on client feedback, marketplace changes, product enhancements, and any other internal or external factors that would affect the client. While there is no standard format or content for a sales playbook, most would include these elements as a starting point:

- Description of the ideal client
- Business overviews of your top twenty-five clients

- Scripted features and benefits of your products and services
- Overview of key competitors and their respective advantages and disadvantages
- Scripted responses to the most common objections
- Typical cross-sell and up-sell opportunities
- Case studies of a broad-range of clients who have successfully utilized your products and services

In addition to the master playbook, successful rainmakers also prepare (i.e., *write*) marketing game plans in anticipation of specific client meetings—similar to what a football coach would create for an upcoming game. This targeted game plan would include such elements as:

- Review of previous dealings with the client
  - Meetings, conference calls, and correspondence
  - Sales—realized and potential dollar value
  - Complaints or kudos
- The client's business environment
  - The competitive landscape
  - High-growth or no-growth
  - Financial stability
  - Scalability
  - Product or line extensions
- Management and key personnel
  - New players or stable roster
  - Decision-makers vs. implementers

- Likely needs and concerns
- Hot buttons
- Meeting specifics
  - Objective of meeting—from your perspective and client's
  - Key questions to ask
  - Logical next step(s)
  - The close

Creating this type of detailed game plan, combined with developing your personal manifesto and master playbook, is hard work. But if rainmaking were easy, it wouldn't be called rainmaking. Indeed, the best rainmakers work so hard at their jobs and improving their performance that the end result appears easy to all onlookers. To quote Vince Lombardi again, "The price of success is hard work." And, to unabashedly quote myself, "it would still be a bargain at twice the price."

ROE #13

KILL THE CAT

Creative insight is the most important asset that marketers bring to the table. And creative insight—driven by wide-ranging and deep-seated curiosity—is the force behind developing and delivering innovative solutions for customer needs. The best marketing happens with a question mark rather than an exclamation point. The trick is to free yourself from self-imposed and externally imposed constraints and allow your mind to wonder, speculate, and hypothesize.

The presence of self-imposed constraints is ironic. Rainmakers are highly intelligent, highly confident individuals; and those are the very traits that drive their success. The flipside, however, is that confidence and intelligence tend to make people highly opinionated—and strong opinions can close people's eyes to other options, perspectives, and opportunities. The best marketers are able to suppress their own beliefs and opinions and observe the world with an almost childlike curiosity and sense of wonder. Rather than grabbing on to an idea or viewpoint and tightening their grip whenever it's questioned, marketing rainmakers do the questioning themselves. If there's a better way to do deliver value or stand out from the crowd, they want to be the ones to discover it. And if there is an untapped need in the marketplace, they want to be first in line to satisfy it.

The externally imposed constraints that limit or derail our curiosity are far more insidious. One of the chief culprits is the American educational system. In fact no less an authority than Albert Einstein, perhaps the most curious intellect of the twentieth century, observed that, "It is a miracle that curiosity survives formal education." The increased reliance on standardized testing and mandated curricula combine to create an environment and mindset that is far more focused on the answer—the one-and-only *correct* answer—than the process of discovery. The result is a system of checkmarks—a focus on simply checking things off a list that the students "know" and can regurgitate on command. Instead of creating intellectually curious minds, our focus as a society is on ensuring that students score high on state-mandated exams, thereby ensuring that the school district will continue to receive state funding. We're teaching kids to pass tests rather than imparting real knowledge.

The other externally imposed constraint on curiosity is our never-ending need for speed. In today's business environment, we want to have answers and make decisions immediately. The idea of true free-flowing brainstorming, combined with intelligently designed fact-finding and thoughtful discovery, is anathema to most organizations. They may give lip service to the concept of creative thinking and thought leadership but, in reality, the process of deliberation is often viewed as a sign of weakness. We're expected to act and act fast. "A poor decision is better than no decision at all" is the mantra of many organizations. This mindset of shortcuts and expedience is largely responsible for the diminishing power and prestige of the United States in the global economy. Ironically, our response is to speed up even more in a futile attempt to make up lost ground. It may be counterintuitive, but the solution is to slow down to speed up. By encouraging and rewarding curiosity rather than stasis and groupthink, we can cure much of what ails American business and, in the process, dramatically improve our marketing efforts and service delivery.

Here's how to build a curious mindset:

- Forget everything you know – Intelligence and functional expertise often serve as blinders and need to be put aside to achieve breakthrough results. Henry Ford, the creative genius behind numerous business and manufacturing innovations, provides the perfect example of how knowledge can get in the way. Ford wanted to protect the passengers in his automobiles by using unbreakable glass on the windows. His engineering staff shook their heads and said it couldn't be done. Ford's response was immediate and succinct: bring me some smart and eager young people who don't know that it can't be done. Those smart and eager young people dove headfirst into the project and invented shatterproof glass. What's the unbreakable-glass project in your industry?

- Open your eyes and ears – The Hollywood producer, Samuel Goldwyn, once noted that, "The harder I work, the luckier I get." Goldwyn was referring to the business world in general, but his words have special meaning regarding the power of curiosity. Many of the indispensable objects we use every day—including Teflon, vulcanized rubber, and Post-It notes— were the result of fortuitous accidents. And they might have remained undiscovered if their "inventors" had not looked more closely at the curious nature of those accidents and extrapolated useful applications for them. Two of my financial services colleagues used this technique to start a booming second business. One of them met an accountant at a cocktail party and, rather than giving the guy the cold shoulder and trying to mingle with the more exciting non-accountant types, he did what every good rainmaker is supposed to do—he asked a lot of questions. He learned that the accountant was a whiz at conducting reverse-audits (which recoup overpaid sales and use taxes for corporations) and wanted to break off and start his own company. Problem was he didn't have access to the C-level executives who make the decision to undertake a reverse-audit and, even if he could get in front of them, his sales skills were lacking. A few more questions—rather than a few more drinks—and a match made in heaven was formed. Opportunity is everywhere if you actively look for it.

- Enjoy the journey – When most people talk about a desire to "travel more," they're not focused solely on a particular destination. Rather it's about the total experience. A trip to France, for example, begins with a brochure at a travel agent's office. Additional research prior to the trip is made with the help of Fodor's guides, Internet chat rooms, and advice from friends and colleagues. The next step is packing in anticipation of fancy nights out and casual afternoons, and tucking away reading material for the long flights to and from. Arrival at the Charles de Gaulle or Orly airports constitutes a baptism by fire ritual that hints at the multiplicity of peoples, languages, customs, and foods you're about to experience. Your small but charming hotel room in Paris, your first meal, your first encounter with a chocolatier, your visits to Versailles and Mont Saint-Michel—all of these things comprise the wonder of traveling to France. Think of it as a corollary of "the whole is greater than the sum of the parts." In our example, the "sum of the journeys is greater than the destination." Exploring the nooks and crannies that surround us can lead to the discovery of a locals-only patisserie or a service enhancement that will leapfrog the competition.

- Be a nuisance – You know those annoying little kids (unless they're your own, in which case they're marvelously gifted) who ask question after question until you reach the bursting point? That's who you want to emulate. To quote Albert Einstein again, "The important thing is to not stop questioning. Curiosity has its own reason for existing." Ask the same question different ways and be curiously surprised by the variety of different nuances embedded in the answers. Ask "why" and "how" long after it's comfortable doing so. Consider the following example and the amount of additional information gleaned by "nuisance" questions—with the end-result being a very specific action rather than a premature close rife with platitudes.

Prospect:	We're looking for a new accounting firm.
Dead-End Response:	That's great because we're one of the best in the area. How soon can we start?
Curious Response:	**Why?**
Prospect:	Our last firm seemed to lose interest in us
Dead-End Response:	That would never happen with us. We pride ourselves on customer service. When can we start?
Curious Response:	**Why?**
Prospect:	I think because we changed our business model pretty dramatically last year.
Dead-End Response:	We pride ourselves on our ability to adapt to the changing needs of our clients. Do we have a deal?
Curious Response:	**How?**
Prospect:	We're now doing most of our business overseas and we wanted help hedging our currency risk.

Dead-End Response:	We have a lot of clients we help with that. Can we get started helping you?
Curious Response:	**And?**
Prospect:	They said they could handle it, but I think they were overwhelmed when it came down to doing it.
Rainmaker Response:	It can be overwhelming, that's why we have a partner who specializes in firms with exposure to foreign currencies. I'll ask him to join us.

A CURIOUS AFTERTHOUGHT

One of the worst things about living in the 21st century is that everything that tastes good or feels good is bad for you. Not so with the processes of curiosity and discovery. Our bodies actually reward us for being curious. The human brain produces additional dopamine when we try new activities and explore our environments. Dopamine is associated with feelings of pleasure, increases general arousal, and enhances the creative juices that drive idea generation. In other words, the more curious you are, the more curious you become.

I liken this *quid pro quo* aspect of curiosity to how I explain the benefits of studying algebra and geometry when my kids complain that "I'll never use any of this in the real world." I agree with them, but explain that the key benefit is not learning algebra but rather learning how to think, where to look, and how to synthesize discrete data points to reach a logical and defensible conclusion. They look at me with blank stares; I trust you are not doing the same.

ROE #14

FUHGEDDABOUT WOULDA COULDA SHOULDA

Marketing is not gambling. Marketing is about growing a business and, accordingly, risks should be minimized and rewards should be maximized. The "Woulda Coulda Shoulda" mantra of the racetrack loser has to be eliminated from every marketer's vocabulary.

"Woulda" looks at the world through the rearview mirror and focuses your attention on yesterday's issues and needs. The end result of this type of thinking will be marketing that does not work for today's customer. It keeps you several steps behind the market and the competition and, at some point in the not too distant future, you'll find yourself so far behind that you will never be able to catch up.

The "Coulda" mindset makes you lose focus on what's best for the client. It focuses almost exclusively on how things could have been better for the company "if only we had" done this or that.

"Shoulda" implies moving away from the integrity of your vision. If something "should have" been done, then it should have been part of your strategic vision. If it wasn't part of your vision then it *shouldn't* have been done. If indeed it *should have* been done and *should have* been part of your vision, then your strategic planning process is flawed and your vision needs to be radically reworked.

"Woulda Coulda Shoulda" represents the antithesis of focus. In most cases it is driven by looking back at what the competition has done and the successes they have enjoyed. The "Woulda Coulda Shoulda" mindset wants desperately to replicate those successes but ignores the fact that the world is changing at light speed. It represents a prescription for failure, and anyone who ascribes to it should be gored by a charging rhinoceros ridden by an invective-spewing hedgehog.

Say what?

As different as they are, rhinos and hedgehogs share a single-minded approach to life that works perfectly for their respective physical and mental capabilities. They are relentlessly focused on survival. Any type of internal "Woulda Coulda Shoulda" debate would be deemed irrelevant because they survived the past— meaning they made the right decision at the right time—and they are now looking forward.

In the business world, rhinos and hedgehogs have been popularized by two eminent thinkers.

Paul Johnson, the British historian and author, wrote an already classic essay for the January 30, 2006 issue of *Forbes*. In "The Rhino Principle," Johnson praises the rhinoceros for its steadfast focus and ability to spring into action whenever it feels threatened: "When [a rhinoceros] perceives an object, it makes a decision—to charge. And it puts everything it's got into that charge. When the charge is over, the object is either flattened or has gone a long way into cover."

There is no second-guessing in the mind of a rhino, nor should there be in the minds of rainmaking marketers. Your line of sight should be precisely framed and unwavering. Johnson says

it best: ". . . if we want to do the big thing, if we hope to leave
a record that will be admired and remembered, we must learn
to distinguish between the peripheral and the essential. Then,
having clearly established our central objective, we must charge at
it again and again until the goal is achieved."

To the rhino, "Woulda Coulda Shoulda" does not exist.
Such a thought process would distract from the moment at hand.
Rhinos don't care about defeating yesterday's enemies, they only
care about today's enemies. By dealing effectively with today's
enemies, they will be better able to deal with tomorrow's as well.
Replace "enemies" with "business issues" and you'll have the
Rhino Principle for rainmakers.

Hedgehogs were made famous by Jim Collins in *Good to
Great* and originally philosophized about by the Greek poet
Archilochus who said, "The fox knows many things, but the
hedgehog knows one big thing." In other words, despite its
cunning and crafty ways, the fox is invariably defeated by the
hedgehog's simple, albeit effective, defense—curling up into a
tight ball with its porcupine-like spikes aimed in all directions.
Collins described the hedgehog approach as such: "Hedgehogs . . .
simplify a complex world into a single organizing idea, a basic
principle or concept that unifies and guides everything . . .
For a hedgehog, anything that does not somehow relate to the
hedgehog idea holds no relevance. . . . [They] see what is essential
and ignore the rest."

As with the rhino, a "Woulda Coulda Shoulda" attitude
would be disastrous for the hedgehog. Remaining focused on the
present constitutes a matter of life or death for the little creature.
A fixation on past opportunities would create huge blind spots,
within which the hedgehog is unlikely to survive.

One could argue that rhinos and hedgehogs occupy a
world far simpler than our own, and thus have an easier time
maintaining focus and discipline. On the other hand, one could
argue that business folks make things far too complicated and

worry too much about things they can't control (i.e., the past). So much time is wasted debating about what should have been done and imagining how wonderful life would be if we only knew then what we know now.

Rainmaking marketers appreciate the past because it provides insight into the future, but they don't dwell on past mistakes or lost opportunities. The only opportunities that matter are today's. Today's opportunities may not be gift-wrapped and labeled as such, but they do indeed hold the key to your success. And while it is certainly easier to look backward with all the acuity that hindsight provides, doing so will only ensure that you'll also be looking backward next year and the year after that. "Woulda Coulda Shoulda" represents a vicious circle that must be broken if true rainmaking and true marketing are to occur.

ROE #15

MUDDY THE WATERS

I wouldn't describe my wife as a crunchy granola type, but she definitely has some New Age vibes going for her. We were recently vacationing on Cape Cod and visited the Heritage Plantation Museum in Sandwich. One of the exhibits is a labyrinth. Now, if you're an uncultured boor like me, you probably think a labyrinth is the same thing as a maze, with tall hedges and a series of false turns and dead-ends designed to confuse and disorient. Not so, my fellow dolt. A labyrinth features a single, albeit complex, circuitous path from the outside to the center—with the same path being used to make your exit. And while hedges are sometimes used to delineate the labyrinth, more commonly the path is distinguished by bricks, crushed stone, or marble (as is the case of the famous labyrinth on the floor of the magnificent cathedral in Chartres, France).

So, as we approached the labyrinth—and the tall hedges I had envisioned were nowhere to be seen—I asked my wife what I thought was a logical question: "What's the point?"

In retrospect, her wifely reply was quite constrained. She rolled her eyes and told me to be quiet, start walking, and clear my mind. She then proceeded to head down the path and I obediently followed.

The good news is that my mind is easily cleared and, within a couple of hundred paces, an amazing thing happened. I began to enjoy the process. My pace slowed and I grew increasingly observant of the contours of the land, the decorative plantings, and even the way the heel, toes, and arch of each foot played their role in moving me forward. And then, in an epiphany of sorts, the theme of this chapter (which at that point consisted solely of a title) came to mind.

I've always been an upfront kind of guy. Cut the BS and get right to the subject at hand. I'm a firm believer that the shortest distance between any two points is a straight line. But as I walked the labyrinth, I realized that I was taking a far more interesting route that offered a greater variety of perspectives than if I had followed a straight-line course from the outer rim to the core. I would have missed a lot if I had simply gone from Point A to Point B. And I began to wonder if the same thing were true of business activities. Does the straight-line approach to decision-making and problem-solving encourage us to jump to conclusions? Does a sole focus on the facts and nothing but the facts cause us to ignore the nuances of a situation? Is the end more important, equally important, or less important than the means?

As a society, we're enamored of quick fixes. We prefer to travel the road that everyone else is heading down rather than its less-trampled counterpart. And we often ignore the caveat that "if something sounds too good to be true, it probably is" and its marketing corollary that "if something appears too obvious, we're probably missing something."

All of this points to a critical element of the hardwired marketing mindset—unleashing the devil inside each of us. Every successful organization needs a strong devil's advocate—someone who can stir things up, muddy the waters, and throw a couple of monkey wrenches into the mix just to see what happens. That role, ideally, should be played by the marketing-minded rainmakers. The most effective and successful marketers function as change agents who question every aspect of their business. They have the ability to view the business from the perspective of a disinterested third-party or, even more valuably, as an aggressive competitor hoping to gain market share. Effective marketers understand that it's their role to lead the organization via strategic insight, not via groupthink and vacuous cheerleading. Insight and clarity are almost always the end result of a devil's advocate debate. If, after you've given the devil his day in court, everything stills looks perfect and you're more resolved than ever to proceed as planned, that's great. But if things look a bit murky, there's still time to tweak and refine to make it perfect—or you may decide to trash the whole idea. Whatever the result, you'll be acting with a far better understanding of what you're doing, why you're doing it, and how it will impact the market as well as the rest of your enterprise.

How to be a Devil

First off, you have to forget your mother's admonition to always be a good little boy or girl and to always say nice things so people "like" you. Being an effective devil's advocate requires a commitment and some sacrifices. You'll piss some people off. You'll ask tough questions that make people squirm. You'll embarrass colleagues who can't answer your pointed questions. In some cases you'll turn articulate orators into bumbling idiots. But, hey, it's all for a good cause. You can't uncover the truth if you're afraid to get your hands dirty.

For those of you who, unlike me, are not natural pains-in-the-butt, here are some ways to kick-start your devilish streak:

- Forget everything – As a rainmaker, you're probably a pretty smart individual. You likely know everything there is to know about your company, your products, your clients, your competitors, and the markets in which you compete. To the devil's advocate, however, that's all meaningless. Make believe you know nothing. Ask the most stupid and most obvious questions—and listen closely to the tap-dance responses they elicit. Your duty as a rainmaker is to ignore the status quo, challenge conventions, and fully align yourself with everyone's favorite economist, John Kenneth Galbraith, who observed that, "The conventional view serves to protect us from the painful job of thinking."

- Assume nothing – Remember my anecdote about walking the labyrinth with my wife? I had assumed that the contemplative activity would be the proverbial crock; and if she hadn't batted her baby blues at me (or, more precisely, rolled them at me), I would have opted to sit on a bench and think about where we should have dinner that night. Instead, I proved my assumption to be wrong (and, in the process, proved for the zillionth time that Laura is my better half). Labyrinths that offer a whole new perspective on things are readily available in every business. Open your eyes to them and your creative and devilish mind will quickly follow.

- If you must assume, assume the worst – While being an inveterate pessimist is a terrible way to live one's life, having the ability to identify and foresee worse case scenarios in one's professional life can prove invaluable. When considering a new project, consider every possible thing that could go wrong. When reviewing promotional material, identify the words, pictures, and concepts that might confuse, anger, or otherwise turn off a prospect or client. When designing a new product, consider the circumstances that would cause it to fail in the market—and what that failure would mean to the rest of your product line and your overall reputation. When I worked at Columbia Funds, one of our star portfolio managers was Ralph Wanger of the Acorn Fund. Ralph also founded and headed Wanger Asset Management and one of the ideas he ingrained in the psyches of his investment colleagues was to always "test for the falsehood." Prior to buying or selling an equity position, the portfolio manager and analysts would be required to argue the opposite viewpoint and determine whether the pro or con argument was more compelling.

DEVILISH QUESTIONS

When words fail you, pepper discussions with questions along the lines of:

- What's the single most compelling reason to do this?

- What happens if we don't do it?

- If we do it, will the competition match us? If so, how fast? And if so, is it still worth doing?

- Are we simply matching the competition or leapfrogging them?

- What specific opportunities are we giving up to pursue this one?

- How will this help us sell more stuff, increase margins, or improve customer satisfaction?

- What's the urgency?

DEVILISH QUESTIONS THAT SHOULD HAVE BEEN ASKED

Just for fun, consider how differently things might have worked out if someone had asked a devilish question within the following companies:

- Coca-Cola – "Is anyone really going to buy New Coke just because it tastes more like Pepsi?"

- Smith-Corona – "Is anyone here worried that personal computers might eliminate the need for typewriters?"

- Gateway Computers – "If our specialty is direct sales via the phone and Internet, does it really make sense to invest in stand-alone retail stores where people still have to wait for the PC to be shipped to their homes?"

- Dean Witter – "Honestly, is anyone going to buy stocks from a guy who works in a booth at Sears?"

- Pets.com – "What does a sock puppet have to do with selling pet supplies?" Or, "What happens if we spend our entire budget on a single Super Bowl ad and nobody notices?"

- United Airlines – "Let me get this straight, we're gonna cut our name in half, call ourselves 'Ted,' offer the same crappy service, and expect to capture market share from JetBlue and Southwest?"

- Arthur Andersen – "Does anyone here really understand how Enron is making so much money?"

ROE #16

Start From Scratch

Zero-based budgeting is fairly common in the corporate world, but "zero-based marketing" is virtually unknown. Zero-based marketing starts with a clean slate and asks questions like, "Why are we doing this?" "What would happen if we didn't do it?" "What else could we do with this investment of time and money?" "What could we do that no one else has ever done?" Every element of every marketing program should have to pass this "opportunity gained vs. opportunity lost" litmus test before being funded and staffed.

Despite what many marketers would have you believe, spending money does not equate to marketing. Successful marketing is focused on increasing revenue and profit. Spending money can help achieve those goals, but not by indiscriminately flinging dollars against the wall to see what sticks. Of course there once was a time when profligate marketing was all the rage. Back in the good old days, marketers could sit in on a budget meeting and have their boss turn to them and ask, "So, Mr. Marketing Director, what are we getting for our gazillion-dollar advertising campaign?" And the marketer would be able to smile and explain that—as everyone knows—half of all advertising dollars are wasted; only no one knows which half. At which point the boss and assorted colleagues would chuckle and move on to the next topic. Nowadays, a comment like that would get you a kick in the butt and an invitation to explore other career options.

In today's world you have to be smart in how you deploy your marketing dollars and resources. While, technically, marketing will never be a profit center on its own, it does have to contribute to profitability, and the best way to ensure that is to start from scratch with no preconceived notions, no sacred cows, and no corporate baggage. Just ask yourself one simple question: "If I were moving across the street and starting my business anew, what would I do differently?" Would I:

- Change my corporate name, tagline, logo, or design template?

- Spend more or less on public relations, advertising, direct mail, sponsorships, or e-marketing?

- Focus on a different niche or multiple markets?

- Hire more technical specialists or freethinking strategists?

- Enter into more or fewer strategic alliances?

- Raise or lower prices?

- Recruit some, all, or none of my current colleagues to come with me?

Despite the fact that there are literally hundreds of similar questions that should be asked and answered, very few initiatives ever start with a truly clean slate. More typically, marketing projects are kicked off with a weak-kneed battle cry along the lines of, "let's see what [*the other guy*] has done." Take a look at the competition's marketing material, advertisements, product specs and design, pricing models, distribution channels, and target audience. At first blush, it sounds like the perfect starting point. See what the other guy is doing so your team can do it better. In reality, however, this type of competitive review leads to me-too mediocrity and, even worse, changes the end game from transforming the marketplace to simply besting the competition. Without repeating the key points of ROE #37: See the Whites of Their Eyes, understanding the competition is important, but understanding the customer is even more important. So start with a clean slate that looks at the world from the client's perspective.

When my business partner, Jane Mancini, and I founded our financial services advisory firm, I-Pension LLC, we consciously and systematically looked for a marketplace opportunity that was being ignored. So, rather than creating a product and looking for a market, we first identified the market and created a service offering that responded to customer needs. We found that the vast majority of people were woefully unprepared and ill-equipped to manage their investment portfolios—a problem that was exacerbated by the almost universal elimination of company-funded pension plans. In addition, most financial advisors wanted nothing to do with the mass market of small investors—preferring to focus their attention on affluent folks with over $500,000 of investable assets. The prevailing belief was that servicing the small investor was an unprofitable, and thus unattractive, proposition. From our perspective, we saw a market with little competition and designed a product that was appealing and affordable to the customer and profitable for us. It wasn't rocket science. We simply looked where no one else was looking.

In the I-Pension example, we certainly benefited from being a start-up. We didn't have to worry about costly infrastructures and entrenched value systems. Our slate was pristine. We could do whatever we wanted. The good news is that, other than Fortune 500 sized companies, the same opportunity can be enjoyed by most businesses. It takes courage and vision, but it can be done. It just can't be done halfway or half-heartedly. There is no such thing as a half-clean slate if you want to unshackle yourself from the restraints of "we've always done it that way" conventional thinking.

To the contrary, the "no one's ever done it that way" approach to marketing and business leads to wildly disruptive rainmaking epiphanies like what Radiohead, the UK-based alt-rock band, introduced with the 2007 release of their album, *In Rainbows*. Rather than selling the album through traditional outlets like Circuit City, Wal-Mart, and Amazon—or even via newer digital distributors like iTunes and Napster—Radiohead invited fans to their web site and offered downloads for whatever price the customer wanted to pay. There was no "suggested retail price" and freeloaders were treated the same as paying customers. The album sold over one million copies in the first month at an average price of $6.00. Customers felt they were part of an elite community and, by selling direct to their audience, the band earned a substantial multiple over what they would have collected if the record company, distributor, and retail outlets all took their cut of the proceeds. In addition, Radiohead's innovative approach generated a massive amount of publicity that drove existing fans to their web site and introduced new fans to their critically acclaimed music. It was a stroke of rainmaking brilliance that started with a blank slate and truly rewrote the rules of music distribution. Other bands will surely follow Radiohead's lead, the old-line record labels will scramble to cut themselves into the action, and the music industry will never be the same—until the next Radiohead wipes the slate clean and raises the bar a bit higher.

Is there a Radiohead-like opportunity in your industry? Before you shake your head and respond in the negative, ask yourself whether you would have gone along with Radiohead's name-your-price strategy. Would you have believed that most people would pay a fair price? Would you have anticipated the millions of dollars of free publicity Radiohead generated?

Similarly, would you have believed that people would willingly wait in line, learn new terminology, and pay three dollars for a venti Starbucks coffee? And would you have believed that people would purchase automobiles sight unseen as they do every day on eBay?

Every industry can support breakthrough thinking. It's the rainmaker's job to provide it.

Section Three

The Tactical Rainmaking Marketer

ROE #17

CELEBRATE SMILESTONES

With so much emphasis on long-term strategies, brand building, and big-picture thinking, it's easy to lose sight of and appreciation for the day-to-day progress we make towards our grand vision. There's even a school of thought that congratulating ourselves on smaller victories would lessen our focus on the long-term goal. Bill Belichick, coach of the New England Patriots and highly respected throughout the NFL as a great strategist and team leader, appears to be solidly in that camp. He never wants to dwell on a victory but instead always points to the Super Bowl as the only "W" that really matters. As much as I admire Belichick and all he has accomplished for New England, every once in a while I'd love to see him, and his similarly discreet players, stand up after a game and shout, "we whupped their scrawny asses good and we'll do it again the next time they crawl into town." Then, after that one indulgent indiscretion, they can go back to their gentlemanly "it's business not personal" ways.

Bill Belichick's stoic approach is especially prevalent in professional services firms where automaton-like behavior is often preferred over flesh-and-blood emotion. But if you really do believe that marketing, at its core, is designed to motivate; and you believe that an emotional connection is the greatest motivator of all; then you need to put aside time to celebrate, encourage, and recognize the efforts and achievements of your colleagues, your clients, and yourself.

The One-Minute Manager, written by Ken Blanchard in 1981 but still highly relevant today, focuses on this idea of "catching someone doing something right" and then recognizing them on the spot. I read the book when it first came out, back when I was a very junior marketer at Wang Labs. Shortly thereafter, I distinctly remember our Group Managing Director, whom I had rarely spoken to, coming into my cube, placing a hand on my shoulder, and telling me—for all my cubemates to hear—what a great job I was doing on a particular project. I remember thinking to myself that he had learned this technique from *The One-Minute Manager*, but that was okay. He was sincere and specific in his praise, and it made my day. Whatever your role or level, try to make someone else's day on a regular basis—and spread the praise around to your colleagues, spouse, children, and friends. And don't forget your clients.

Here's a great example of how one entrepreneur wins loyalty points by celebrating his clients' small victories. I recently produced a music CD and one of the distribution outlets was CDbaby.com, a self-described "little online record store that sells albums by independent musicians." CDbaby was founded in 1998 by Derek Sivers, a musician turned rainmaker, and has paid over $50 million in royalties to its artists. Every aspect of Derek's approach to business celebrates and encourages his clients, including his royalty checks:

Hey Philip

I just sent you a direct ACH deposit for $50.73. If the bank numbers you gave us are correct, it should appear in your account in the next two days.

Yes it's good to get paid paid paid paid for making music!

I hope I write you a million more checks.

I hope you write a million more songs.

I hope you get a million more fans

who give you a million kisses

all because of CD Baby.

Ciao!

Derek Sivers

When you experience CDbaby—whether as an artist or a customer—it becomes very clear that Sivers had a visceral vision of what he wanted to build from the first day he opened his online storefront. Most importantly, he had the courage and discipline to pursue that vision one step at a time. It's easy to picture Sivers smiling to himself as he crafted the royalty communication shown above or wrote the equally jovial confirmation emails that are sent to customers when purchasing CDs or designed the whimsical CDbaby web site. Each of these steps represented a milestone in Sivers' business plan, and by turning them into "smilestones" he further motivated himself to keep at the hard work of building a business. That's what rainmakers do.

Joseph Priestley, the eighteenth century English philosopher, once commented on Sir Isaac Newton that had we "traced all the steps by which he produced his great works, we might see nothing very extraordinary in the process." That comment aptly describes *kaizen*, the Japanese philosophy of continuous improvement driven by small but steady steps. What Isaac Newton and Japanese powerhouses like Toyota and Sony have in common is a well-visualized long-term goal supported by an equally clear visualization of how to get there.

A vision is not the same as a daydream. There is no magical snapping of fingers or clicking of heels that can immediately deliver one's vision fully realized and ready to go. The process of vision-actualization is a continuum. Think of it as a chain, with each link representing a milestone and each link making the chain longer, stronger, and more versatile. Each link constitutes an entity unto itself and is essential to the efficacy of the final product, but it's pretty much worthless on its own.

That's why we tend to ignore milestones and don't give them their celebratory due. Most milestones are indeed relatively "worthless on their own" (e.g., breaking ground for a new building, filing an affidavit, or designing a logo). If the projects were to end there, nothing of lasting import would have been accomplished. You'd have a big hole in the ground, a few sheets of paper imprinted with heretofors and forthwiths, and an all-hat-no-cattle business.

Milestones are important because they represent the means to a specific end. And rather than contributing to a loss of focus on the big picture, milestones help to make the big picture more real and serve to tightly connect people to the grand scheme. They provide a deeper understanding of what success will look like and the effort that will be required to achieve that success. Milestones are very similar to the anticipatory build-up to events like a high school prom. The anticipation is often more exciting than the real thing. And while you would never skip or otherwise disavow the real event, it was in the planning and anticipatory phase where the "heavy lifting" occurred and strongest memories were implanted.

In the business world, it's way too easy to focus on weaknesses and missteps rather than strengths and victories. It's part of human nature. Notwithstanding that most performance appraisal systems are designed as coaching and developmental tools, the manager and subordinate typically spend the vast majority of their time on the single "needs improvement" rating rather than the dozen "above average" ratings. The Pollyanna in you will argue that this is a good thing because it's focused on improvement, perhaps even continuous improvement. The counter-argument is that we simply don't spend enough time recognizing and leveraging all the good stuff we do. The good stuff is expected. That's what we're paid to do.

The cliché about the chain being only as strong as its weakest link became a cliché because it's true. The best way to ensure that even the weakest link is as strong as possible is to recognize its value from the outset and then reaffirm its value when completed. Take a moment to celebrate the small accomplishments before moving on to the next. That's what rainmakers do. And that's what good marketing is about.

ROE #18

IGNORE THE BLISS

Notwithstanding all that Smilestones schmaltz in ROE #17, no one really cares about what you accomplished yesterday. Bruce Springsteen captured the sentiment perfectly in "Glory Days," his ode to middle-aged mediocrity when "time slips away and leaves you with nothing, mister, but boring stories of glory days."

Success is something we all strive to achieve, but it has a dark side as well. Success can breed complacency. It's easy to get fat, dumb, and happy as we rest on our laurels. A pat on the back for a job well done is great—but stay smart and stay focused, and you'll also stay well ahead of the pack.

If only it were that easy. As part of my career in marketing, I've hired and listened to countless dozens of professional speakers. These are typically folks who are regulars on television and radio, have written a book, have held senior-level positions in the government or corporate America, won an award, surmounted some obstacle, or did something else that qualifies them to charge $25,000 for a one-hour speech. They are highly

skilled and respected individuals, experts, and champions in
their respective fields, but when they take the stage you literally
want to shoot yourself. They move around the stage in quite a
life-like fashion, talking, gesturing, and chuckling along with
the audience. But it's a sham. A charade. They may have done
something at some time that wowed someone, but that day is
long gone. Now, they're simply going through the motions,
playing a role. Words are being spoken, but the speaker is not
engaged or engaging. The jokes are mechanical and the heartfelt
sentiments are cloying. The whole thing comes across like a
comeback tour for a 1980s glam band (i.e., it's being done solely
for the money with no pretense of adding anything of value).
They're reaping the rewards today for what they accomplished in
the past.

I don't mean to single out professional speakers because this
tendency to coast once success is achieved is surprisingly—and
disturbingly—rampant. It stems from feelings of self-satisfaction
and enchantment with one's press clippings; and it manifests itself
in a lack of preparation for meetings, overconfidence in one's
abilities, overreliance on past techniques and strategies, disregard
for the thoughts and insight of others, and obliviousness to all
of the preceding. It's all driven by delight in having achieved
the pinnacle of success—a level of personal success that cannot
possibly be surpassed.

When you're the best, you're the best. Except when you're
Tiger Woods.

As overused as they are, sports analogies do work well to
bring certain business concepts to light. I think it's because of the
hardwired mindset of professional athletes that is best expressed
via the adage that "Amateurs practice to get it right; professionals
practice to never get it wrong." You need to look no further than
Tiger Woods, who may very well be today's best athlete in any
sport. After winning several majors and climbing to the number
one ranking in the world, Woods completely retooled his swing.

The naysayers clucked when Tiger stumbled out of the box with his new technique and showed himself to be mortal after all. Within eighteen months of introducing the "new" Tiger, however, he again began to dominate his PGA colleagues and continued his attack on the record books. The moral is that if Tiger Woods needs to continually review and enhance his skills, everyone does.

Here are some easy techniques to retool your professional swing and ensure that you stay at the top of the rainmaking game:

- Treat existing customers like prospects

- Treat employees like you're still recruiting them

- Create an agenda for every meeting and identify exactly what you want to accomplish, then grade yourself afterward

- Document your professional accomplishments on a timeline to see if major wins are as frequent today as they were in the past

- "Google" yourself periodically to see if your online identity and listed accomplishments reflect what you're doing today or what you did last year

- Approach every day as though it's your first day on the job

- Conduct a 360-degree performance review to gain perspective on your performance from peers, superiors, and subordinates

- Conduct skip-level meetings with the people who report to your direct reports

- Write your obituary including only those successes that were achieved from this day forward

- Learn something new every day

- Teach something new every day

- Talk with someone new every day

ROE #19

Stick It

Stickiness is the new black; and sticky has replaced permission, viral, one-to-one, and word-of-mouth as the newest buzz word of marketing. And it makes sense because stickiness—the ability to help people remember and be emotionally engaged by what they see, read, or hear—is key to effective marketing. In truth, the idea of stickiness gets at the very heart of what good marketing is all about. But it's hardly a new concept.

Way back in the time of Moses, the biblical writers recognized that brevity was key to ensuring the stickiness of a message. As a result, despite the citation of sixteen "imperative statements" in the Exodus and Deuteronomy passages relating to the commandments, the Bible specifically refers to *ten* commandments. Various religions combine the sixteen imperatives in different ways, but there is clear unanimity in the need to reduce the total to a more manageable, memorable, and authoritative-sounding number.

During the presidential campaign of 1840, William Henry Harrison used the slogan, "Tippecanoe and Tyler Too," to remind voters that he was the hero of the Battle of Tippecanoe and his running mate for Vice President was John Tyler. And just as with more recent political sound bites like "Read my lips" and "It's the economy, stupid," the sing-song phrase helped with the election.

In 1904, the Campbell Soup Company introduced an illustration of two cherubic children for a trolley car advertisement. This was one of the first uses of a brand "spokesperson." The "Kids" became widely popular and serve to this day as iconic images of the value of a warm meal and good nutrition for children.

In more recent years, the stickiness meter has gone off the charts with advertising mantras like Wendy's "Where's the beef?" campaign. Rather than stating that their hamburgers were X-percent larger than the competition's, Wendy's demonstrated in a powerful, funny, and memorable way that the size difference was plainly visible for anyone to see.

And is there anyone in the lower forty-eight over the age of thirty who can recite the words "Plop, plop, fizz, fizz" without following the beat of the Alka-Seltzer jingle or refrain from adding the "oh what a relief it is" lyric? It's become part of our core memory.

The more jaded of you may question what relevance any of this has to the world and work of rainmakers. My response is that the stickiest phrase of the 1990s was coined by a rainmaking defense attorney, Johnnie Cochran, when he held up a glove and said, "if it doesn't fit, you must acquit." He was marketing his case to the jury, and he wanted his message to stick. (Unfortunately, he was successful.)

Regardless of what business you're in, you communicate for a reason. You want your message to be understood and remembered. You want your words to resonate and reflect positively on you and your business. And you want to motivate your audience to take action. That's what stickiness can do, and that's why it needs to become an integral part of everything you do and say.

HOW TO STICK IT GOOD

While stickiness is something of an art, it can be learned. It also has the additional benefit of being fun. Who wouldn't enjoy being able to turn a phrase that captures people's attention and positively affects the way they view you and your product or service offerings? There is no downside with stickiness. So, with no pretense of being all-inclusive, here are some easy-to-implement ways to add stickiness to your day-to-day communications.

- Tell stories – Stories are the single greatest contributor to stickiness. Indeed, if you consider all the examples included in the previous section you'll see that each tells a story. (See ROE #44: Tell a Story Worth a Thousand Pictures, for more examples regarding the stickiness of stories.)

- Include visuals – A good friend of mine, let's call her Trisha (since that is her real name), is a top salesperson of alternative investment products—i.e., hedge fund strategies offered in retail mutual funds. Trisha always begins her presentation with two images side-by-side. One image shows the luxury and pampering of an airline first-class cabin and the other shows an overcrowded, cramped, and largely ignored coach cabin. As her audience absorbs the images, Trisha reminds them what it feels like to be in coach, wondering what happens behind the curtain that separates them from the first-class passengers. She then makes a comparison to how individual investors look enviously at endowments, hedge funds, and other institutional investors and wish they could share in the wealth. "Well," says Trisha, "with my company you can, because we bring first-class to coach. We can deliver institutional-style investment strategies to the small investor." Her clients always remember the "bring first-class to coach" imagery, and she always remains at the top of the sales charts.

- Get specific – Gabriel Garcia Marquez, author of *One Hundred Years of Solitude* and one of the truly great writers of the twentieth century, once told the *Paris Review* that, "If you say there are elephants flying in the sky, people are not going to believe you. But if you say there are four hundred and twenty-five elephants in the sky, they probably will believe you." Specificity demonstrates confidence in the information you're sharing, and makes it more meaningful and memorable. You would never tell a friend that you just bought a sports car; rather you'd name the make and model, and maybe even the color (e.g. "I bought a red Porsche Boxster just to prove I really am having a mid-life crisis."). As you market your firm and yourself, then, avoid the generalities that we all tend to use and replace them with concrete facts and figures. Don't say cost-effective when you can say twenty percent less expensive than ABC or XYZ. Don't say industry-leading when you can say "ranked first" in something by someone. And don't ever allow clients to decipher vagaries on their own.

- Make it rhyme – There is something comforting about rhymes due to their cadence and childlike simplicity. Most importantly, however, rhyming serves as a strong mnemonic device because of its repetitive framework that inextricably links two ideas or images (e.g. "doesn't fit" and "must acquit"). The rhyming technique has less universal application to the business of rainmakers, but as Johnnie Cochran demonstrated, when it works it can work wonders.

- Get a laugh – Humor is a great way to capture attention, help ensure that your message is heard, and build rapport with your audience. And I'm not talking about telling jokes or being clownish. Focus instead on incorporating a clever turn-of-phrase into your day-to-day dealings with clients and prospects. A local tutoring firm, that is always being challenged by Kaplan and other larger competitors, uses a simple catchphrase to point out the need for its services: "4 out of 3 kids have problems with fractions." It's hard not to smile at that, and equally hard not to enroll your kids right on the spot.

- Twist it – Familiarity does indeed breed contempt, but it can also come in handy when you're fighting for mindshare. The trick is to not rely on clichés but instead give well-known phrases a twist that makes them more meaningful and memorable. A former colleague, and one of the best platform presenters I've ever witnessed, practiced this technique whenever he wanted to highlight the popularity of a particular idea or action. Rather saying "9 times out of 10" he would say "9 times out of 11." While the math didn't quite synch up— the latter wording snapped people to attention and underscored the point he was making. Similarly, an online direct marketer expresses the power of Internet advertising by positioning his service as "word of mouse."

- Surprise them – People love surprises and tend to remember them long after their mundane counterparts are gone and forgotten. One of the best ways to accomplish this is through the juxtaposition of two seemingly opposites—as exemplified by the marketing campaign that Metamucil launched in 2007. As a fiber supplement originally designed to relieve constipation and encourage regularity, Metamucil was positioned far away from the glamour industry. However, with a campaign that urges consumers to "Beautify Your Inside" and offers the benefit of "drop-dead gorgeous guts," Metamucil is reminding people that beauty truly is not skin-deep, but rather is the end result of a healthy and balanced lifestyle. And that's a message that should resonate strongly with the target audience of thirty- and forty-something women who want to look good and feel good.

- Analogize – People learn and remember complex concepts best via analogies. Here's a personal example. I've worked in the financial services industry for over twenty years but still find much of our terminology confusing. I had a particularly difficult time understanding the various measures of risk that were bandied about. One of the most common risk measures is standard deviation, the technical definition of which is "a measure of the dispersion of a set of data from its mean." Clear as mud, right? Here's an analogy that a colleague created that makes it a lot more understandable. There are two families, Family A and Family B. Both have three children. The Family A children are ages 10, 12, and 14. The Family B children are ages 2, 12, and 22. So in terms of the mean and median ages, the two families are identical. However, in terms of dispersion from the mean, the families look quite different. Without getting into the mathematics of it, Family A has a standard deviation of 1.63 while Family B's standard deviation is 8.16. I still can't do the math on my own, but I'll never forget what standard deviation is all about.

THINGS THAT UNGLUE

Like every powerful force, stickiness has its own set of antagonists that must be banished before they unglue your best efforts.

- Superlatives – In a world where "unique" no longer means "one of a kind" but rather refers to anything that is slightly different from the ordinary, superlatives have lost their impact and credibility. Does a company exist whose mission statement does not reflect the desire to become the "premier provider" of one widget or another? Do phrases like "outstanding customer service" and "world-class facilities" create memorable images or positive feelings to anyone? Avoid superlatives to build a super brand.

- Industry jargon – Everyone knows you're an expert in your field. Prove you're a smart expert by translating jargon into plain English.

- Exclamation points – The superlatives of punctuation have no place in marketing!

- Bold capitalized letters – **RATHER THAN CALLING ATTENTION TO YOUR MESSAGE, BOLD AND CAPITALIZED LETTERS SERVE NO PURPOSE BUT TO ANNOY AND MAKE THE TEXT DIFFICULT TO READ.**

- Weasel words – Coined by Theodore Roosevelt and named after the weasel's ability to suck out the contents of an egg and leave the empty shell intact, weasel words drain the life out of communications. Weasel words are typically used to purposely confuse the reader, to appear less threatening and thereby soften one's image, or hide the fact that the speaker truly has nothing of importance to say. Weasel words and phrases to avoid include:

  - "Studies have shown . . ." (I read it on some twelve-year-old's blog)

  - "To tell you the truth . . ." (because I haven't been truthful thus far)

  - "I think I have something you might be interested in . . ." (because I really don't have the time or inclination to delve into your real needs)

- "As everyone knows . . ." (but I like to hear myself talk so I'm going to tell you anyway)

- "I'm not supposed to tell you this . . ." (but no one would ever tell me anything truly confidential so no harm can come from it)

ROE #20

SHORTEN UP TO SWEETEN UP

In 1863, Abraham Lincoln composed the Gettysburg Address using only 272 words. Today, there are 401 words on a bag of potato chips; 1,153 words of assembly instructions with a child's tricycle; 2,900 words in the average annual report "Chairman's Letter" to shareholders; and around 10,000 words in a typical mutual fund prospectus.

Enough said.

POSTSCRIPT

(My editor, who is evidently a stranger to irony, felt a 55-word chapter really didn't do justice to the issue at hand, so here is a bit more insight—which I promise to keep brief.)

First off, given the choice, I would highly recommend that, whenever and wherever possible, you draw upon all the literary powers bestowed on you by the good Lord (or whatever holy or non-holy entity to whom you attribute your prowess in crafting a well-turned phrase) to strive to use as few words as you possibly can (especially those of the highfalutin' multisyllabic variety) to express the central thought that you want your reader to take away from his or her encounter with your written, oral, printed, or digital promotional communications. In other words, less is more.

This less-is-more concept, however, runs counter to everything human. As a species, we love to hear ourselves talk. We trade quantity for quality, and we confuse store-bought erudition with insight. (Ernest Hemingway once made this comment about William Faulkner: "Does he really think big emotions come from big words? He thinks I don't know the ten-dollar words. I know them all right. But there are older and simpler and better words, and those are the ones I use.")

We talk for the same reason we snack on junk foods—to fill the empty spaces. And just as we binge eat, we talk long beyond what's necessary. In fact, the less people know about something, the more they tend to talk. Think about it. You've probably done it yourself. When you're asked a question you're thoroughly prepared to answer, odds are that your response will be precise and succinct. If you don't know the answer, but won't admit it, your answer is likely to be a long, rambling mumble that creates confusion and erodes confidence.

Long-windedness has nothing but downsides:

- We reveal more than the audience wants or needs to know

- We open our words to misinterpretation

- We raise additional issues and concerns in the mind of the client or prospect

- We make something that's simple sound complicated

- We bore the audience to death

Most importantly, the more words we use, the less memorable they'll be. We live in an age of taglines and soundbites. Few people would argue the merits of such a superficial society—but it is our reality. Challenge yourself to use the eraser as often as the pencil, and pare down your client communications to their essential ingredients. You'll be amazed how much more you can say by leaving out the excess verbiage that clouds rather than clarifies your message.

Going back to the Hemingway theme, he was once challenged to write a short story in as few words as possible and came up with this: "For sale. Baby shoes. Never worn." Faulkner couldn't have said it better using a thousand words.

POST-POSTSCRIPT

(Irony of ironies, either my editor was right, I'm on a roll, or I've fallen in love with my own voice.)

When it comes to successful marketing, the short-and-sweet principle refers to more than just the language we use. The most egregious affronts to professional sensibilities occur in the design of sales and marketing materials; and the culprit is desktop publishing software. It is far too easy for people who can't even draw a straight line to gleefully design customer newsletters, multipage brochures, and, gulp, web sites. Most amateur graphic designers have never met a font they didn't like. They combine serif, non-serif, bold, italic, condensed, uppercase, and underlined typefaces to such excess that their promotional materials resemble ransom notes. They then throw fuel onto the fire by the haphazard and injudicious use of color. The result is something that resembles a gaudy Christmas tree decorated by a herd of blind jitterbugs.

And most insidiously, just as we talk to fill up the empty spaces, untrained designers prefer to fill every inch of paper or pixel with their "don't forget I was here" handiwork. Just as a well-timed pause can dramatically impact your spoken words, well-placed white space can make the truly important words and images jump off the page (far more so than bright red, bold and underlined text followed by an exclamation point could ever accomplish). Professional designers treat white space as a design element—and you should as well.

ROE #21

FACE THE FACTS

Some marketers believe you should never let the facts get in the way of a good story. If a statement sounds good, they don't care if it doesn't really say anything of substance. Their job is to sell the sizzle and let someone else worry about the steak. Marketing is all about creative license; let the bean counters worry about the facts.

Rainmaking marketers believe otherwise. To them, facts constitute the backbone of a good story. Without them, stories are amorphous and blob-like. Facts provide stories with the ability to stand on their own and, in the process, transform puffery into profundity and drivel into differentiation.

Rainmaking marketers understand that you market emotionally but sell factually. Here's the how and why.

A common theme woven throughout the "52 Rules of Engagement" is that people make purchase decisions based on emotional connections and how the product or service makes them feel (or how they anticipate the product or service will make them feel). Interestingly, however, people often rely on facts to help justify the purchase decision. Think of it as a form of rationalization. You fall in love with the redesigned Audi TT and have to have one. You love the way it looks and handles, and the way you feel when driving it. That's the emotional connection. In addition, however, it gets great gas mileage for a sports car (so it's environmentally correct), has all-wheel drive (so it's safe), and even has a back seat (so it's practical). You've now created a solid fact-based foundation to support your purchase decision. You've satisfied both your emotional and intellectual needs. All that's left is to sign the paperwork.

As with all elements of communication, a hierarchy exists among facts. The more precise the fact; the more powerful its effect. Precision sells and engenders confidence. Whereas politicians are often faulted for being wishy-washy, it's extremely rare that anyone would be called out for being too precise in their communications. Precision creates understanding and strong visualization. Say the word "car" and nothing in particular comes to mind. Say "Porsche" and distinct imagery immediately appears. Say "red Porsche Boxster" and you can be sure that you and your audience are seeing the exact same thing.

Facts also provide a context to help people understand a vague concept. The Apple iPod, for example, comes in a 160-gigabyte version. On its own, a 160-gigabyte hard drive constitutes a fact; however to someone like me, it has little meaning. It sounds huge, and I assume I can load it up with every song I own. Besides its generic "hugeness," I have no context for assessing how amazingly large the iPod hard drive is. Apple understands that and tells me the iPod can hold 40,000 songs. That's a pretty good factoid in itself, but Apple goes one step further and tells me, I "could drive from New York to San Francisco twenty-five times and never hear the same song twice." Now that's huge. It's also the kind of factual sound bite that captures people's attention and sticks in their memory.

The best way to reap maximum benefit from factual statements is to provide a supporting visualization of the fact. Going back to the iPod example, 40,000 songs is a hard image to visualize, whereas a cross-country road trip is something most of us have daydreamed about. Words and pictures reinforce each other and make the resulting message extremely powerful. Canon perfectly exploits this approach with ads for their cameras and lenses. Canon positions itself as "the number one choice of professional sports photographers and photojournalists" and the "official camera of the NFL." Whether by plan or luck, the telephoto lenses on Canon cameras are white rather than the traditional black of their competitors. As a result, instead of just stating the percentage of sports photographers that use Canon equipment, the ads depict actual photographers at work on the sidelines of actual games. These images show a sea of white lenses only rarely interrupted by a black lens. This visual is seen not just in Canon ads but is also repeated and reinforced every time the television camera captures a player scoring a touchdown or running out-of-bounds because, invariably, there's a white-lens-sporting photographer right there to catch the action. Canon has created a situation whereby their paid advertising generates a ton of free advertising. And just as Nike has the swoosh logo that says Nike even when the name is not spelled out, Canon has the white lenses that reinforce its position as the camera of choice even when its name is nowhere to be seen.

The power of the iPod and Canon examples derives from specificity and precision. Unfortunately, most of the marketing we experience is of the "new and improved" variety (i.e., when you have nothing to say, say it pretty and say it loud). The AMC chain of movie theaters offers the perfect example. AMC expresses its competitive advantage via this tagline: "Experience the difference." Despite the fact that AMC probably paid a brand consulting firm many thousands of dollars to develop this positioning, it would be hard to imagine a less engaging and less meaningful tagline. What's truly sad, however, is the U.S. Patent and Trademark Office lists eighty-eight other companies who have filed trademark applications for that very tagline or some slight variation. In addition to movie theaters, "Experience the difference" serves as a trademark for dental floss, jewelry stores, kitchen appliances, cut flowers, and wax candles. A tagline that can be used with so many different types of products cannot, by anyone's definition, be unique or compelling. "Experience the difference" cannot help people visualize the benefit of visiting the respective movie theater or buying from the candle maker. It is puffery at its worst. And it needn't be that way. If any of these companies truly offer a distinguishing experience, they should tell the customer what the difference is. Don't let them guess. Tell them. And by telling them, you create a more receptive mindset that will more quickly recognize and appreciate the difference. Coyness has no place in marketing. Coyness doesn't sell. Facts sell.

ROE #22

SAY NO TO YES BUT

An "oxymoron" refers to the combination of two incongruous or contradictory terms (e.g., jumbo shrimp or deafening silence). And while the ubiquitous "yes but" response to new and different ideas may not fit the dictionary definition, I'd suggest that it is indeed the most diabolical of all oxymorons. Delete it from your vocabulary and a whole new world of rainmaking opportunities and possibilities will magically appear in front of your eyes.

At its worst, the yes-but phraseology represents a closed-minded, knee jerk response to anything that hasn't been done before—or that the rebutter didn't think of first. Typically it will be supported by a comment that while the idea sounds good in theory, it wouldn't work in practice. From a linguistic standpoint, even its construction is devilish: It begins with a positive affirmation ("yes, that is a good idea") and ends with a cutting off at the knees ("but it won't work for reasons that I understand but which escape the abilities of your feeble mind").

Yes-but thinking is driven by a variety of factors that, if left unchecked, will stifle innovation and creativity. To wit:

- Overconfidence – Yes-but aficionados tend to love their all-knowing selves. Ideas that don't sync with their personal beliefs are deemed foolhardy and foolish. Plus, if someone else came up with an idea that was superior to my own, that would make you better than me, which is an unacceptable conclusion that can only result from faulty inputs and thought processes. Confidence is a requirement of rainmaking; overconfidence, however, quickly morphs into arrogance and ultimately leads to blindness and deafness to the thoughts and ideas of others.

- Lack of confidence – New ideas, by definition, have not been done before; and that can be terrifying to the less resolute marketer. It's easy to attend too much credit to the marketplace and competitors and assume that if an idea were really good someone else would have already thought of it. How could a dolt like me, the thinking goes, have a breakthrough epiphany? How? By not succumbing to the tyranny of yes-but naysaying.

- Internal focus – The vast majority of yes-buts come from colleagues, not from customers. The best way to defeat internal yes-buts is to focus externally on customers, both existing and prospective, as well as the marketplace as a whole. Internal yes-but heads are focused on the status quo. Rainmakers focus on changing the way things are today, and building a better experience for tomorrow. Do the right thing for your external customers, and your internal colleagues will inevitably drop the yes-buts and hop on the rainmaking bandwagon.

- Fear – We fear the unknown. New ideas, no matter how compelling and seemingly idiot-proof, represent a risk. To many people, risk is a four-letter word to be avoided at all costs. I come from the investment world where risk is an important consideration in stock selection and portfolio management. Risk is something to be managed, not avoided altogether. A risk-free investment portfolio would be limited to low-yielding securities like T-bills and would not deliver the returns required by most investors. A risk-managed portfolio, on the other hand, uses diversification to moderate the riskiness of any one holding. This same risk management approach works for other industries as well. Don't yes-but an idea because it involves risk. Instead, take time to specify the risks and quantify the rewards. There is a point at which risk levels are too high to justify the payback, and that's okay as long as a fair and honest assessment was conducted.

- Non-suspension of disbelief – Does anyone really believe that Superman was able to disguise himself as Clark Kent with little more than a pair of glasses and a shy personality? Or that a small boy would or could conceal a space alien in his bedroom as Spielberg presented in *E.T.: The Extra-Terrestrial*? Or that Jack Bauer survived past the very first episode of *24*? The suspension of disbelief is a critical component in the development and enjoyment of many of the world's most beloved novels and films, and it is equally important in the creative process that drives innovation in the business world. Creativity is the lifeblood of marketing. It enables marketers to see and make connections among and between diverse products, audiences, distribution channels, and platforms. Yes-but thinking throttles creativity and the ability to suspend disbelief. When allowed to flourish at the extreme, yes-but thinking suspends belief in human's ability to accomplish the unlikely (ordering a pizza via a text message from a cell phone), the improbable (turning a nerdy, Subway-eating Jared into an iconic everyman), or the impossible (landing a man on the moon). Yes-but is a limiting attitude that has no place in a rainmaker's repertoire.

- Indecisiveness – At its core, yes-but represents an institutionalized delay mechanism that is often stated as "yes, but have you thought about…?" The not-so-between-the-lines meaning is that you don't have all the facts so you can't possibly make an informed decision. It's a ploy that works better when counting beans rather than making rain.

- Consensus – The worst type of indecisiveness revolves around building consensus—making sure everyone is "onboard"—and is typified by comments like "yes, but have you gotten input from finance (IT, operations, manufacturing, or the boss's brother-in-law)." Management by consensus constitutes corporate suicide or, in the best-case scenario, corporate mediocrity. As General George Patten phrased it, "No one is thinking if everyone is thinking alike."

IDENTIFY YOUR OWN YES-BUT

In addition to eradicating yes-but from your personal vocabulary, you need to remove it from others' descriptions of you. None of us is perfect. We all have quirks and idiosyncrasies, and there are some things we're good at and other things we're not so good at. The latter are the facets of our being that populate the "yes, but" statements that clients, colleagues, friends, and family make about us. For example:

- "Yes, John is extremely talented, but he's late with every project."

- "Yes, Susan has great rapport with clients, but she treats her internal support team like indentured servants."

- "Yes, Eric is really great with numbers, but he refuses to help out with anything unless there's something in it for him."

It would be very easy to ignore the yes-but aspects of our own personal and professional lives as trade-offs for the value we add via our strong points. But the easy way is rarely the best way. Rather than accepting your yes-buts as the necessary evils of your genius, tackle them with the same commitment and urgency with which you approach the core of your rainmaking skills. Turning a weakness into a strength is infinitely more satisfying that bulking up an existing strength. Turning a yes-but into a yes-and is rainmaking nirvana.

ROE #23

Sweat Like a Pig

In fairness to swine the world over, pigs don't actually sweat. Like most mammals, pigs do have sweat glands but in insufficient quantity to properly regulate body temperature. Their cooling technique of choice is wallowing in mud. Nonetheless, in mindful repudiation of the "Face the Facts" ROE, I choose to not let the facts get in the way of a good headline. (See ROE #52: Burn This Book for more ROE-busting inspiration.)

Marketing is composed of a thousand little things that—in the aggregate—capture the hearts, minds, and wallets of your prospects and customers. Rainmaker marketing is about getting all those little things done effectively *all the time*. It's about sweating the big stuff and the little stuff and everything in between. Apple, Target, and Starbucks are masters of this approach with their single-minded focus on creating a positive customer experience from start to finish. The good news is you don't need multimillion dollar budgets to create a similar experience for your clients. You just need to pay attention to the details.

There's a restaurant in Minneapolis that could serve as the poster child for attention to detail. As with most upscale restaurants, the tables are set with traditional white napkins. When guests take their seats, however, the waiter will gracefully replace the white napkin with a black one for those diners wearing dark trousers or skirts. Why? Because white napkins often leave lint marks on dark-colored clothing. It's a small but meaningful touch that sets the tone for a memorable dining experience.

Switching napkins is a very visible sign of attention to details, but there are also many behind-the-scenes opportunities to contribute to a positive customer experience. The most neglected customer communication vehicles are business forms like applications, invoices, statements, and the like. Most businesses, and most of the sales and marketing types within those businesses, view these communications as administrative nuisances that represent bureaucratic red tape rather than marketing opportunities. Wrong. I'll never forget requesting a change of beneficiary form from my insurance agent. The life insurance contract was for one million dollars, and the form I received looked like it had been photocopied a million times. The text was smudged and difficult to read, and the whole form was misaligned on the page—a mistake that had probably been made several thousand copies ago but which no one had found troubling. It struck me that neither the agent nor the insurance company viewed my million dollar policy as particularly valuable. And, as a result, it lessened their value in my eyes.

Nothing is too little or too insignificant to be safely ignored. Once you start ignoring the small stuff, your definition of "small stuff" will inevitably creep upward and firm-wide quality will begin to spiral downward. And even if you are able to maintain high standards of quality on the "big stuff," your clients' perception will forever be altered if you give short-shrift to the small stuff. As every restaurateur knows, if the bathroom is dirty diners will think the kitchen is dirty as well.

Everything matters because it's impossible to know what will matter most to any particular customer. Every interaction with a customer constitutes a potentially defining moment of truth. It could be the simplicity or complexity of your voicemail system, the way your receptionist welcomes visitors, your office furniture and artwork, the scope and usability of your web site, the timeliness and readability of your invoices, how you introduce yourself, your email template and signature, your cell phone ring tone, your clothing and posture. Everything your clients and prospects read, see, hear, feel or touch from you should be carefully thought-out and choreographed. Nothing should be left to chance. Nothing should happen by accident.

Put it all together and it's really quite simple. Sweat the big stuff and the small stuff, and attracting and keeping customers will be no sweat at all.

A No-Sweat Corollary

It's critical that you never let your prospects and clients see you sweat. Do all your sweating behind tightly sealed doors in the privacy of your home and office. Follow the carpenter's adage to "measure twice, cut once" in everything you do.

Rehearse presentations aloud. Videotape yourself and review with a critical eye. Put yourself in the place of your audience and honestly assess if your key messages are popping out and likely to be retained.

Arrange seminar seating so you, as the presenter, can look everyone straight in the eye.

Prepare for meetings the same as you would for a formal stand-up presentation. Develop a meeting agenda. Rehearse your opening comments. Define what you want the meeting to accomplish.

Edit telephone and voicemail scripts so every extraneous word is deleted.

Before using an application form or questionnaire with customers, give it to a spouse or friend. Time how long it takes to complete the form. What areas were confusing? Did some questions have insufficient space to write the answer? Did the sequence make sense?

Enter your office reception area and take a seat. Is the chair comfortable? Would it be comfortable for a woman wearing a skirt? Would it be comfortable for an elderly, overweight, or infirm visitor?

Identify your most important product, service, or marketing piece—then visit your web site and see how many clicks it takes to find it.

Rewrite and reformat your billing statements and customer agreements as though they were brochures or advertisements. Then figure out how to incorporate some of the marketing tone and wording to improve the existing statements and agreements.

Script and edit everything. Arrange and rearrange everything. Test and retest. Practice and rehearse words and tone. Reflect on and review every possible interpretation, misinterpretation, and nuance. Squint, stare, gaze, and focus from every possible perspective. Repeat from the beginning.

The more time you spend upfront and the harder you work at planning, rehearsing, and critiquing, the more confident, comfortable, and natural you'll appear to your clients—and the more you'll stand out from the competition.

ROE #24

LOSE YOUR HEAD

Ludwig Josef Johann Wittgenstein hardly sounds like the name of a wild and crazy guy. Nonetheless, the Austrian philosopher had a softer side and was a strong proponent of a light-hearted approach to life and work. "If no one did anything silly," he observed, "nothing serious would ever get done."

David Ogilvy, widely recognized as the Father of Advertising, shared Wittgenstein's belief in the power of levity. "The best ideas come as jokes," he said. "Make your thinking as funny as possible."

Despite the urgings of Wittgenstein and Ogilvy, there remains considerable resistance to humor in the workplace. It's viewed as inappropriate and wasteful. Even in cases where humor is accepted within the confines of the corporate office, it is frowned upon when dealing with customers. Evidently interactions with customers require a game face—stern and omnipotent, albeit in a friendly way—so as to inspire confidence and certitude. It's okay to smile at and with customers, but that's the limit. Anything more and the whole foundation of American capitalism will come crashing to the ground. It's a patently ridiculous perspective. Virtually every business succeeds or fails based on the strength of its relationships with customers—particularly in industries pervaded with look-alike products and services. Plus, if you consider that the end-customer is pretty much always a man or woman, and men and women both rate a sense of humor as the number one trait they value in friends and mates, it's logical to conclude that business relationships are far more likely to advance to the next level if nudged along by a bit of humor and a fun vibe.

Marketing in particular is supposed to be fun. Sure it's essential that marketing be viewed as a business within a business—but that doesn't mean it should take on the persona of finance or systems (not that there's anything wrong with finance and IT people). Sales and marketing types receive a form of corporate dispensation for their more gregarious outlook on the world, and thus have a ready-made platform from which to spread mirth and good will. Not using that platform to its fullest advantage constitutes professional malpractice and provides entrée for the sales and marketing team down the street to reap the benefits that you've abdicated.

The only potential downside of integrating humor into your marketing efforts is that you're not as funny as you think you are and your attempts at humor fall flat. (I'm purposely excluding the downside of using sexist, racist, and similar forms of antisocial humor because you already know better than that.) The kind of humor we're talking about does not hinge on telling jokes and possessing the perfect timing of a stand-up comedian. Rather, it's more of an atmospheric humor—a willingness to poke fun at our own foibles, to use self-deprecating humor, and an ability to enjoy the human side of business. And no industry or line-of-work is inherently precluded from incorporating humor. Clearly you need to pick your spots and avoid trying to inject humor where not appropriate, but you also need to understand and appreciate how to use humor to defuse tense situations and difficult discussions. (Note: The more squeamish of you may wish to skip the next few sentences.) Several years ago, as I approached the ripe old age of fifty, I was having my annual physical when the doctor began putting on the dreaded rubber gloves. As I cringed and braced myself, he loudly snapped the rubber glove on his wrist and cheerfully said, "If it's Tuesday it must be prostate exam day." Now it's not the funniest line ever uttered, and he certainly used the same line on every trembling middle-aged man he examined; but it made me chuckle and let me know he empathized with my nervousness. His humorous remark helped make the best of an uncomfortable situation, and that gets at the heart of what humor in the workplace is all about.

Humor creates a form of community in which we can laugh together. It breaks down walls and creates an environment more open to the natural give-and-take rhythm of conducting business. Humor relaxes people and encourages them to let go of their natural defenses and engage in dialogue. The ultimate goal of marketing is to grease the skids for the sales team, and there is no better way to accomplish that than via the use of humor. Even if you ignore all the benefits humor delivers to our interactions with customers, a healthy sense of humor makes our own jobs more enjoyable as well. Richard Branson exemplifies this belief with his personal philosophy: "I don't think of work as work and play as play. It's all living." Humor is an important part of living and should be an important part of work as well.

HOW TO GET SERIOUS
ABOUT HUMOR

Humor provides a complementary attribute that can get people to look at you—and appreciate you—in a whole new way. Here are some simple ways to dip your toe in the humor well.

- Blog – If you're one of the dozen or so professionals who don't yet have a personal blog, now would be a good time to start. Blogging provides a simple and less intimidating way to let clients see your lighter side—especially if you focus on areas outside of your specialty. A stock broker, for example, who makes his living providing advice on the market, uses his blog to dispense advice of a different variety—what movies to see and which to avoid. He's a longtime movie buff and his reviews are purposely full of malapropisms and double-entendres that are frequently more entertaining than the movie itself. An accountant, who grew up wanting to be a rock star, has a weekly blog in which he posts rewritten lyrics of popular songs incorporating tax-related themes (e.g., "When Irish Eyes Are Smiling" becomes "When Uncle Sam is smiling / Well you know that's bad for you / Cause he'll take the shirt right off your back / Then he'll want your socks and shoes."). It's not Gershwin but it elicits a smile.

- Humorous surveys – People enjoy being asked their opinion and seeing how they compare to the "norm." Rainmakers can use this to their advantage and create a "user community" by conducting non-business related surveys of their client list and sharing the results, anonymously of course, with the participants. Who could resist responding to a questionnaire that asks you to name the one cartoon character you'd want to have as a companion on a desert island, the one song you can't resist singing along to, the super hero you most identify with, and your most embarrassing faux pas?

- Professional jokes – Every profession has its own litany of jokes and gibes. Rather than having them be the unspoken 800-pound gorilla in the room, share them yourself as an ice breaker. The self-deprecation will go a long way in building rapport, capturing attention, and establishing a relaxed tone.

- Quotations – A former colleague was a master at integrating
  humorous quotes into often deadly PowerPoint presentations.
  His rationale was simple: "The less I say the smarter I sound."
  This technique is easy to implement—but ensure that the
  quotes are related to your subject matter so that they reinforce
  your overall message.

ROE #25

SLOW DOWN TO SPEED UP

It's a business truism that you never seem to have time to do it right but always have time to do it over. Unfortunately, in a world where perception is reality, the kinds of problems that arise from not taking time for thought and reflection can be fatal. Problems like flawed strategies, wasted resources, missed opportunities, and weak execution can all lead to customer disenchantment and business failure. Rainmakers can often perform miracles, but undoing the damage of a botched opportunity is usually impossible.

We live in a world of increasing immediacy and decreasing turnaround times. "I want it now" is less of a command and more an expectation of our daily lives. And while I have never been one to advocate slow and ponderous decision-making and thought processes, speeding through life and business creates problems whose remedies often escape us. We don't know how much better a project could have turned out if we had allowed ourselves to take another day and consider other alternatives. The rush to get something out the door is too often focused on checking it off our to-do list and moving on to the next item. Quality and excellence, while given lip service, are often pushed aside and usurped by expediency. An all-too-common mantra of the mid-level worker is, "I'd rather get it wrong and be on time, than be late and get it right." And they feel that way because that's what they sense from their superiors. It's an attitude that embraces and seeks out shortcuts. Instead of measuring twice and cutting once, we eyeball the dimensions and hope for the best.

Speed has replaced quality as the catchword of today's business world. It's an addiction that can destroy the mind, body, and soul of a company or practice. The vast majority of businesspeople believe they're too busy and don't have the time to do everything they have to. To counter that, they approach every task like a hamster on a treadmill—their arms and legs are moving, their fingers are typing on keyboards, their tongues are flapping into cell phones, but they never seem to make progress. The faster they go, the more static they become. They have a continual sense of urgency that seems to apply equally to large tasks and small—from budgeting and checking email, to employee coaching and ordering take-out. When everything is important, nothing is important. Similarly, when everything is urgent, nothing is important.

Urgency is critical to success in virtually every business and industry but, like everything, it has a time and place. Patients appreciate a sense of urgency in the emergency room but not during a routine check-up. In sports, nothing is more urgent than a football team's two-minute drill when time is running out and the game is on the line. Because football players are finely tuned and highly trained athletes, they often run the two-minute drill to perfection, leading the more casual observer to question why they don't run the two-minute offense for the whole game. They don't because they can't. It would be counterproductive.

The pace and demands—both physically and mentally—are too grueling and exhausting to even be contemplated for an entire game. In business, as in football, you need to pick your spots. You need to continually manage the play clock—slowing down and speeding up as necessary. Sometimes you execute the two-minute drill and sometimes you consciously try to shorten the game. When the ball is in your hands, you call the plays and control the tempo. If slowing down will deliver better results, that's what you do. And when the situation calls for a more urgent approach, you can pick up the pace accordingly. Slow and steady and fast and furious both have their place in sports and business. Focus on the intended outcome to determine your game plan, and do not equate speed with efficiency. It's often the complete opposite.

Slowing down is also invaluable in its ability to reveal the invisible or capture the elusive. About ten years ago I was heading up marketing for a multinational insurance company. We were introducing a new lineup of variable annuity products and we were struggling to find a strong name that had relevance and staying power. We came up with dozens of good ideas; but whenever we checked the names against the USPTO trademark database, we found that they had already been taken. After considerable whining—and frenetic searching through thesauruses, Latin dictionaries, and encyclopedias of Greek and Roman mythology—my wife finally told me to quit obsessing and take a different tack. She told me to take a deep breath and think about things I enjoyed—like cars, wine, and horse racing. Recognizing that Laura is the smartest person I've ever known, I took her advice. I poured myself a glass of Chianti, picked out a couple of books on automobiles and horse racing from our family room bookcase, and sat down in my favorite leather recliner. My feet were up and my mind was open. I remember reading an essay about the great filly, Ruffian, and thumbing through a history of Porsche in America. The two hours spent sipping wine and browsing through books were so delightful that I didn't even mind that they didn't result in a name. At least not on the spot. The next morning I was driving to work when it hit me. *Futurity*. Futurity is the name of a horse race in which the competing horses were nominated prior to birth or during the year of their birth. In other words, it's a commitment made to an event happening in the future—highly relevant to a product line designed to help people save for and prepare for retirement. I called my boss, the president of our company, from the car, explained the idea, and got her just as excited as I was about the potential of the Futurity name. And it was all because I took the time to slow down.

Taking time to take your time delivers another benefit as well. It helps ensure you are aligned with your client or prospect. Business relationships, like all interpersonal relationships, take time to seed and blossom. Problems arise when one party wants to move faster than the other. One party thinks the other is cute and fun to hang out with, while the other is planning a dinner party with parents and talking about moving in together. Suddenly, a relationship with a lot of potential is kaput. Speed, in this context, is presumptuous and does indeed kill. Jumping to the close too quickly at a sales meeting, assuming that clients fully understand the implications of everything you've talked about, and believing that smiles and nodding heads constitute affirmation are equally suicidal. Rainmaking marketers focus on the client and continually adjust their tone and tempo to match the client's need and comfort level. Moving too quickly, however, reflects your needs, a state of mind that your clients will sense and use as a reason to look elsewhere for the satisfaction you could have provided had you only paused for quiet reflection.

ROE #26

Don't Just Because You Can

I was recently driving down a suburban street near my home when I saw a middle-aged couple jogging together. Now I'm sure they are very nice people—intelligent, kind, and charitable—but, try as I might to defeat it, a heartless thought kept running through my mind: "Just because you can wear Spandex doesn't mean you should."

This "Don't Just Because You Can" caveat also rings true for businesses—though it is somewhat counterintuitive. Companies are in business to grow, and growth is often fueled by new initiatives. That reality, combined with the fact that everyone is always looking for the next big thing, creates a tendency to throw a lot of stuff at the marketplace and see what sticks. (Please don't take offense but, in large organizations, it is often the rainmaking sales types who drive this approach.) New products are often used as a corporate crutch—for example, "if we only had XYZ we could double sales." In all likelihood, the exact same thing was said about product or service "ABC," which is languishing in your warehouse or forgotten in the marketplace.

The unfocused, shotgun approach to product development almost always leads to disaster or, if not disaster, higher costs and lower margins. Shotgun marketing forces companies out of their sweet spot. Rather than operating from a position of strength and dominance by focusing on your core competencies, shotgun marketing levels the playing field and eliminates your competitive advantage. It's a lot like the story about the man who bet $100 against all takers that he could beat Tiger Woods. After the stakes reached several thousand dollars, an incredulous young girl asked the man how he intended to beat the great Tiger Woods. The man's response caught a lot of people off-guard. "I'm going to play him at tennis," he said.

Ironically, the biggest contributor to the shotgun approach to marketing is the desire to please the customer and to give them everything they want (with the arrogant presumption that they're going to want it from you). This act of trying to be all things to all people weakens and dilutes your brand positioning and, by its very nature, leads to a lack of focus. This was the downfall of one of the great American brands: Sears. Flush with money from the boom years of the 1950s and 1960s, Sears diversified into the brokerage business, real estate, credit cards and, before anyone had ever heard of America Online, Internet access via the short-lived Prodigy service. It was only after significant retrenchment that Sears avoided bankruptcy, but the firm grasp that Sears held on the American pocketbook was forever lost.

The intelligent approach to growing a business or professional practice is to identify your number one strength and your most noteworthy personal trait. Determine precisely what it is that you do that adds unique value. Write it down and edit out the extraneous stuff that is administrative or technical. What's left is your niche, a niche you can and should own.

It sounds easy but the proverbial fly in the ointment is that most high-powered business people don't like niches. They feel confined by niches. They want to think bigger because bigger is better. Niches are for the less visionary. They represent a compromise or, even worse, a capitulation that one has achieved all that he or she is capable of. Niches are for losers.

The classic example of this niches-are-nowhere attitude comes from Gerber, one of the most long-lived and beloved brands in the world. In the early 1970s Gerber introduced "Gerber Singles"—small servings of fruits and vegetables packaged in the exact same jars as the firm's baby food, but for adult consumers. From the corporate perspective it made perfect sense. Gerber could use the same bottlers, the same food processing equipment, the same suppliers, and the same distributors. The profit margins would be enormous. How could it fail? Well, to the rest of the western world outside of Gerber's corporate headquarters, the idea of grown-ups eating from a baby food jar seemed positively ludicrous—let alone having to stand in line at a grocery store and have the cashier and all onlookers peg you as a pathetic loser. Gerber owned a niche and should have continued to expand their business by focusing on the nutritional needs of infants and toddlers and making childcare easier for parents. Instead, Gerber pursued an opportunity just because they could and didn't take the time to consider all the reasons why they shouldn't.

The widespread nix on niches provides fascinating insight into the entrepreneurial mind. Despite considerable lip service being given to the dangers of "being spread too thin," businesses consciously (albeit unconscionably) choose that route every day rather than be "left behind" in a niche. Guy Kawasaki, one of the original Apple Macintosh "evangelists," refers to this predilection as "The Kiss of Yes" in his highly readable *Rules for Revolutionaries*. Rather than saying no to a new feature, application, or market, ambitious business people prefer to say,

"Yes, we can do that." Were they to think it through, however, they would realize that "Yes, we can do that" is the same as saying "Sure, we can derail our strategy, shuffle our priorities, and incur additional expense on the off-chance that there are a few other knuckleheads like you who would buy XYZ from a company that specializes in ABC." So, instead of saddling yourself and your firm with a no-win headache, amaze your client with a response like, "Yes, I can see why you would want XYZ, but rather than having us reinvent the wheel, I'd recommend that you speak with So-and-So LLC who specializes in XYZ." Your client will be delighted to have experienced a real-life *Miracle on 34th Street* moment and will benefit from access to specialized XYZ expertise. Any fears you may have that So-and-So LLC will steal your client's ABC business reflect infantile paranoia and have no place in rainmaking thought processes. To the contrary, it is far more likely that you will have increased client satisfaction and loyalty tenfold—and will likely get some referrals for ABC-focused work from So-and-So LLC.

That's how rainmakers think and how they become rainmakers.

They choose what they do and what they don't do—and "could" and "should" are never synonymous.

ROE #27

SHOW THEM THE MONEY

When I was a kid growing up on Long Island, there was a New Jersey-based clothing store that ran late night radio ads promoting two-for-one specials, discount financing, and similar come-ons—all accentuated by their "Money Talks, Nobody Walks" tagline. And in 1996, the premaniacal Tom Cruise introduced the "Show me the money!" catchphrase to the American lexicon. In both cases, the underlying theme is that dollars make people pay attention—and when it comes to rainmaker marketing, showing clients exactly how much they can save or how much extra they can earn by working with you will make the difference in closing the deal or walking away empty-handed.

In today's marketplace, most customers are fixated on costs. If you're presenting from a pitch book or RFP, prospects will invariably jump to the end to see what it's going to cost. You can't control that urge, but you can control the messaging around the stated cost. You do that by providing two costs—the upfront cost (i.e., the price you are charging for your product or service) and the payback cost (or the price after applying cost-savings or revenue-enhancements). Mercedes-Benz and Honda have been hugely successful with this approach in two quite different segments of the automobile market. They have highlighted the five-year "total cost of ownership" of their cars against key competitors in their respective categories. The conclusion of these comparisons is that while the initial price might be a bit higher, the greater residual value dwarfs that difference in the long-term. It's a key selling point drilled into every Mercedes and Honda salesperson from coast to coast.

As a rainmaker, your job is to deliver a similarly powerful message to your clients and prospects. It sounds hard until you consider that everything that everyone does in every business is designed to add to the top and/or bottom line. You're selling something of value, and you have to be able to describe that value in a compelling and memorable way. Most importantly, you have to be able to describe it in terms of dollars and cents. There are several different ways to approach the task of assigning a dollar value to your intangible products or services. Here are some of the most common and easily implemented techniques:

- Time is money – Peter Sachs is a highly regarded architect in the western suburbs of Boston. Most of his business comes via referrals from satisfied clients, so it's infrequent that he gets involved in competitive bidding situations. Nonetheless, Peter, who has owned his own construction company and still drives a Ford F-250 to prove it, always talks to new clients about how he can translate time savings into cash savings. His construction experience gives him street credibility with contractors and enables him to speed construction time and minimize delays. From there it is easy to calculate actual savings for clients who are carrying bridge loans or need to rent temporary housing.

- Pick your spots – Market Metrics is a market research firm that provides detailed information about customer needs and behavior—and then assesses the comparative strengths and weaknesses of a company's direct competitors. Steve Delano, president of the firm, has been able to grow the business without discounts or other incentives by focusing on the sheer magnitude of dollars spent on sales, marketing, and service. For a relatively tiny percentage of a company's distribution budget, Steve provides insight into how their money can be spent more wisely. Sometimes, for example, a budget increase in one area can pay huge dividends and be offset by cost reductions in areas viewed as less important by customers. It's the budgetary version of the "work smarter not harder" mantra.

- Now or later – Tom Harrington is an attorney specializing in municipal law. His firm serves as town counsel for three Massachusetts towns and also handles project work for several dozen others. Budgets are always at the forefront of town politics, and cost is an issue with every project. Tom's success is due in part to his focus on a "you can pay now or you can pay later" approach to business. Based on his extensive experience, Tom can point to numerous situations where a $5,000 upfront investment in legal advice prevented or could have prevented six-digit legal bills. A safety net of that magnitude is very appealing to elected officials.

- Quid pro quo – My financial services advisory firm, I-Pension LLC, offers professional money management to 401(k) plan participants for a flat fee of one dollar a day. To most people, a dollar a day sounds like a good deal, but we make it even more compelling by describing other ways they might choose to spend that money—for example, buying one Milky Way candy bar or half of a Starbucks tall latte. Those simple illustrations drive home the cost-effectiveness of the program, and make it hard to say no.

- See the future – Hockey great, Wayne Gretsky, has been famously quoted as saying, "I skate where the puck is going to be, not where it has been." As a rainmaker, the best thing you can do for your clients is to follow Gretsky's lead and provide a glimpse of the future and a game plan for getting there— along with a monetized version of "what's in it for me." Financial services research firm, FRC, markets many of its studies using this very approach. A recent FRC report, for example, focused on the market potential for college savings plans. Assets in this relatively new market segment had grown to over $100 billion by 2007, with continued double-digit growth projected for the future. Investment companies who established themselves in this space only had to capture single-digit market share to reap significant benefits. By hinting at the size of the market opportunity, FRC consultants had great success in selling the detailed research report.

- More for less – While outsourcing has become increasingly popular in corporate America, the need remains to justify the upfront cost, explain the long-term savings, and demonstrate the added value. Several years ago, I managed a group that provided centralized marketing communications support to our various business lines. We worked on a chargeback system that billed an hourly rate for everyone from the production assistant to our creative director. Some of the business line managers complained that it would be cheaper for them to hire their own marketing teams. I relished the opportunity to respond to that objection. I'd begin with their annual outlay. Let's say it was $200,000. I would immediately concede that they could hire three mid-level marketing project managers at $50,000 each plus benefits. The difference, however, in "outsourcing" to my department was that they would have access to fifteen different individuals whose base salaries ranged from $40,000 to $125,000, and whose specialized skill sets ranged from copywriting and graphic design to public relations and meeting planning (not to mention the executive-level oversight that I provided). If that wasn't enough, I pointed out that if one of their three "dedicated" employees were to leave they'd be operating at a 66 percent staffing level, whereas if one of my folks left, we'd still be at a 93 percent staffing level. This usually stopped them in their tracks and is an approach that is easily translatable to most professional services.

A CONTEMPLATIVE FOOTNOTE

I was always taught that it was rude to discuss money in public—especially with perfect strangers. So I feel compelled to add another perspective to this chapter. And rather than relying on my own limited intellect, I'll use the words of some of the brightest minds of the recent and distant past.

Let's start with Ayn Rand, author of the greatest capitalist novel of all time, *Atlas Shrugged*, who offered this warning: "Until and unless you discover that money is the root of all good, you ask for your own destruction." Rand's quote gets to the heart of why we—and our clients—value money. Money is not an end; it's a means. And it's not dirty unless it's used for dirty activities.

Jonathan Swift, of *Gulliver's Travels* fame, offered similar insight: "A wise man should have money in his head, but not in his heart." Swift is talking directly to rainmakers with this quote. Rainmaking marketers need to fully understand all of the financial implications and ramifications of their products and services. And the more they can communicate those implications to prospects and clients, the more successful they will be. The key is to use money as an analytical and informational tool rather than an emotional one.

Henry Ford is customarily direct in stating his personal belief: "The highest use of capital is not to make more money, but to make money do more for the betterment of life." As rainmakers, we have an awesome responsibility. We serve as role models. We set a tone for colleagues, clients, vendors, friends, and family. And our words and actions can help pave the way to a better life for all.

H.L. Mencken, the free-thinking satirist, comes at it from the opposite direction: "The chief value of money lies in the fact that one lives in a world in which it is overestimated." Mencken points to the delicate and critical balance between valuing a dollar for what it represents versus what it can do. At the extreme, dollars represent self-indulgence, arrogance, and flagrant disregard for society at large and the greater good. When properly valued and used as Henry Ford advised, dollars can make a difference far beyond our personal and professional purview. Think of it as rainmaking for the global community—and help it become a reality instead of simply a nice turn of phrase.

Section Four

The Customer-Focused Rainmaking Marketer

ROE #28

Walk a Mile in Your Customer's Shoes—*Backwards*

In today's highly competitive marketplace, you can't truly know your customer simply by walking the proverbial mile in his shoes. You need to take a giant step backward and understand why the customer started walking in the first place. You need to determine his intended destination, as well as the myriad twists and turns that ultimately got him to your doorstep. In short, you need to practice needs-based marketing.

Over the years, lots of people have talked about the concept of needs-based selling. Too often, however, it's simply a contrivance designed to lead the customer to agree that he indeed has a need for the cookie-cutter solution that the salesman ever-so-conveniently happens to have in his hip pocket.

Needs-based marketing takes a polar opposite approach. It has no preconceived notions and no ulterior motives. It focuses on creating a mindset in which you truly put yourself in the place of your customer. Needs-based marketing helps you identify with your target customers and then deliver whatever they need, whenever and wherever they want it, and in whatever form they desire.

Accomplishing that requires focus. A focus on what's important—*not* what's important to you, but rather what's important to the customer. A focus on identifying the core message that will actively engage the customer and determining the key element of that message that makes it vitally important to him.

Consider this real-life example. You're creating a business-to-business direct-mail campaign, and you're starting with something as basic as a promotional postcard announcing an enhancement to one of your flagship products or services. Your target audience consists of existing customers (i.e., people who already know you and who have previously chosen your product over the competition). Relative to most of what you do in marketing, it's a lay up.

Now put yourself in the place of your customer and picture the given postcard arriving in his inbox. At this point, you've begun walking in your customer's shoes—so pat yourself on the back. But before you reach for that postcard and consider what your customer's reaction to it might be, take a step backward. Picture the customer's desk. See his inbox piled high with memoranda, expense reports, trade magazines, and dozens of promotional mailers from companies just like yours. Your first challenge centers on creating a postcard that will stand out from the reams of junk mail that have simultaneously landed on your customer's desk. But you can manage that because, like all good marketers, you know the basic tenets of eye-catching design. You know to focus on the benefits of your product rather than the features. And you know enough to include compelling copy that answers the age-old question of "what's in it for me?"

The problem is that, thus far, you've only taken one step back in your customer's shoes—whereas you need to go all the way back. "All the way back," of course, is defined differently for every customer—but what's a minor technicality like that among friends?

So how do you go all the way back? You do it not by focusing solely on what will catch the customer's eye, but by identifying the focal point of your customer's eye. You must make an all-out effort to experience not only what the customer is experiencing today, but also what he has experienced in the days, months, and sometimes, years before your paths crossed. And you must be able to answer questions like these:

- What is the customer's specific role in his company?

- What is your product's role in his job and in his company?

- Has your product changed your customer's life in any way? How and why? For good or for bad?

- What prompted the customer—or his company—to select your product originally?

- How have his needs—and his company's needs—changed since that original sale?

- How has the market changed?

- How have the competition's products changed?

- And how does he view all of this change? Is it a positive or an annoyance? Does he long for the good old days, or is he excited about all that the future holds?

Consider also that products and services are typically purchased to solve a problem. For example, weekend hackers buy $500 drivers to eliminate a slice or hook. Middle-aged men trade in their Japanese sedans for German convertibles because they have a problem with getting old. And purchasing managers buy new software programs because they have a problem with expenses, data integrity, timeliness, or headcount.

Whatever business you're in, your marketing efforts will be much more effective if you view yourself as a problem solver—and thus prepare yourself to ask and answer a series of questions like:

- What is the nature of your customer's problem?

- How long has he suffered with it?

- Does he know he has a problem—or is it up to you to point it out? (Conversely, does he purposely choose not to acknowledge his problem—thereby making it foolhardy for you to point it out?)

- Is the problem of his doing or has he inherited it?

- What is his motivation to solve the problem?

- And does his motivation coincide with his company's motivation?

Once you can honestly and confidently address all these questions—and dozens of similar ones—you can accurately determine the customer's true needs. Armed with this level of customer knowledge and insight, you can then develop a promotional postcard that will indeed jump out of the customer's inbox and onto your bottom line.

On the other hand, the knowledge and insight you've gained may convince you that a postcard is the wrong medium after all. You may decide that an email, phone call, or personal visit would prove far more beneficial. Or perhaps a seminar or webinar aimed at that particular customer, as well as like-minded customers and prospects, would provide a more effective means to educate and motivate.

Obviously, you can't conduct this level of analysis for every single customer—and I'm not advocating the concept of one-to-one marketing at its most extreme. What I do advocate is an extreme focus on an outward-directed mindset. How much your customers know about you is far less important than how much you know about them. You need to know your customer better than he does—and better than your competitors do.

So while your competitors are walking a mile in the customer's shoes—you do the same thing, only backwards. You'll end up in two different places—but you'll have the more valuable vantage point by far.

ROE #29

REJECT IOUs

Have you heard the saying that "No one cares how much you know, until they know how much you care"? It's a truism that is particularly relevant as you create marketing programs and develop lasting relationships with clients. And it's a truism that can be boiled down to three letters—"I.O.U." Above all else, whatever you do in rainmaker marketing, never place I over you.

Think about every way you communicate with your customers and the content of each of those communications. Then ask yourself this simple question: "Is this an *I* topic or a *You* topic?" If it's the former, then you've fallen into the old trap of focusing on features. You're spending too much time talking about how great you, your product, or your company is. You're taking an egocentric approach to relationship-building and—unless you dramatically change your approach—you'll be awarded an honorary doctorate from the kamikaze school of rainmaker marketing.

"I" topics by definition are narcissistic. They're also self-destructive. Most marketers and sales people have the mistaken belief that the best way to stand out from the competition is to spell out each and every way that *their* company is different and better. The reverse is what actually happens. The more we talk about ourselves, the more we look, feel, and sound like the very competitors we're trying to disparage. We think we're being articulate in a visionary sort of way, but the only vision the client sees is clouded with eerily familiar platitudes.

"You" topics, on the other hand, are focused on the customer's needs and the benefits accrued by utilizing your product or service. The thing to keep in mind is that customers— even the most difficult and least profitable of them—are human life forms. And like all humans, the only thing they enjoy more than talking about themselves is having someone else talk about them. Talk to them in a way that helps identify their specific need and—instead of offering a cookie-cutter solution—talk to them about specific ways you can solve their problem and help achieve their objective. In the process you will create a friend—and a client—for life.

Dale Carnegie, perhaps the only motivational author worth killing trees for, captured the IOU ROE perfectly with his observation that "You can close more business in two months by becoming interested in other people than you can in two years by trying to get people interested in you."

If there's one profession that lives and dies by the IOU approach, it is medical professionals. Their expertise is usually taken for granted, so they don't have to waste time proving their intellectual worth. Their diplomas are hanging on the wall and their credentials are inextricably linked to their names. And because their own success hinges entirely on being able to "feel their patients' pain," they can focus intently on the client without waging an inner debate on "how am I doing?" or "is it time for the close?" or any of the countless other I-centric inanities our minds can dream up.

So that's great news for physicians, but what about the much larger group of rainmakers and service professionals who don't practice medicine? My advice is to follow their lead. Business pain is just as real and debilitating as physical pain. Clients come to you to ease the pain. They know the symptom and are turning to you for the cure. It's your job to diagnose the cause, offer a prognosis, and recommend a treatment. Think of yourself as a business doctor. Your clients cannot flourish without your help. They *need* you—but they remain the center of attention.

Utilizing the IOU approach to think like a business doctor is much like an intellectual form of Aikido, the Japanese martial art. While many of the martial arts are focused on kicking, punching, and overpowering opponents—similar to what most business meetings are designed to accomplish—Aikido takes the opposite tack. It uses an opponent's own weight and energy to gain an advantage. It is practiced and methodical, but at the same time fluid and effortless. It's a thing of beauty that focuses on "You" to achieve what "I" want.

So start thinking like a doctor of business Aikido, and the next book on rainmaker marketing will feature your name as the author (though I hope you mention me in the foreword).

IOU TIPPING POINTS

Here are some tips for identifying "I" or "You" topics:

- "I" topics are transactional. "You" topics are relationship-builders.

- "I" topics are generic. "You" topics are personalized.

- "I" topics are used by salesmen. "You" topics are spoken by friends and trusted advisors.

- "I" topics are disingenuous. "You" topics inspire trust.

- "I" topics attract customers. "You" topics attract clients.

- "I" topics bore. "You" topics engage and excite.

- "I" topics are arrogant. "You" topics are empathetic.

- "I" topics emphasize your knowledge. "You" topics demonstrate your understanding.

ROE #30

ACT BIG, FEEL SMALL

What do customers want more than anything? It's being able to deal with a big company that feels like a small company. That combination of attributes offers the best of both worlds—the peace-of-mind that comes with Fortune 500 status and the personalized service of a mom-and-pop operation. As a rainmaker it's your job to deliver what the client wants, and this particular request is eminently doable. Plus, it's fun.

The first thing you have to do is rid yourself of the perception that bigger is always better. Bigness envy leads to snap decisions and short-sighted vision. Looking back on the dot-com bust of 2000–2001, many of the firms that went belly-up actually had good ideas that could have succeeded. Unfortunately, the mantra of these young firms was to GROW BIG FAST. Their goal was not to change the world or add real value to their customers' lives. Instead, they simply wanted to get big enough to support an IPO and cash in. That's not a business plan; it's a pipe dream stoked with something stronger than tobacco.

There is no shame in remaining a small business. Smallness brings with it several advantages. Small companies are less bureaucratic and, therefore, more nimble, flexible, and responsive. They have interesting personalities and character. They engender increased loyalty because they are perceived as a team of people rather than a faceless corporate monolith. They can be more focused and specialized. They are more creative and innovative because they have less corporate baggage. Most importantly, they are closer to the end customer.

Smallness is an advantage to be leveraged and provides an opportunity to employ a form of corporate Aikido whereby you use the bigger player's perceived strength to enhance your own position. Here are some examples of perceived big-company strengths that can be used to your advantage:

- Lots of people – The most obvious benefit of working with a larger company is its ability to throw more people at a particular project or service. The flipside is that clients will often never work with the same person twice. Partners and senior managers will typically show up for the initial meeting and never be seen or heard from again. With small firms, the partners and senior managers will be there from start to finish. Similarly, inbound calls to a large company are typically handled by the next-available customer service representative. Small firms have the advantage of employing dedicated service reps who handle all communications with their assigned clients and build personal rapport that enhances customer satisfaction and loyalty.

- The best and the brightest – With their deep pockets and fancy offices, larger companies are often thought to attract and employ the most talented staff. In reality, large-company cultures often breed groupthink and a sense of entitlement among staff members. Small companies, on the other hand, are more likely to attract creative thinkers who disdain the very thought of big-company bureaucracy and who will work their proverbial butts off to prove their worth.

- More knowledgeable – Large firms are assumed to know what they're doing and what they're talking about. But as discussed elsewhere in this book, technical knowledge is becoming more and more of a commodity. Small firms can set themselves apart by highlighting their depth of knowledge regarding the client's business and industry. Specific knowledge beats generic knowledge bake-off after bake-off.

- Instant credibility – The reputations of large companies precede them and effectively grease the skids to closing a deal or getting an assignment. In reality, however, clients hire people not companies—and there is a big difference between corporate credibility and personal credibility. The representatives of many large companies often forget this, and they approach client and prospect meetings with a blasé attitude, presuming that the business is already theirs. They mistakenly believe that corporate credibility can overcome a lack of personal credibility. Smaller firms can beat the behemoths at the credibility game by stressing their personal experience and relevant credentials. Instead of dropping the names of trophy clients and high-profile assignments, small firms can point to real-life examples of how they helped specific companies—similar in size and nature to the prospect—solve problems similar to the case at hand.

- Superior technology – It seems logical that larger companies would have access to and utilize the latest cutting-edge systems. In truth, large-company systems requirements are so massive that they are often several years and several versions behind anything even approaching state-of-the-art technology. Small company systems are far less likely to be bound by the constraints of legacy systems and more likely to be able to deliver the benefits of new technology to their clients.

- One-stop shopping – Clients are often attracted to larger firms because of the appeal of having multiple specialties under one roof. The small firm can counter this all-in-one approach, and often better it, by building a network of subject matter experts that can be brought in for specific assignments. This type of network can easily be positioned as a handpicked all-star team, as opposed to the client having to settle for whomever the larger firm happens to have on staff.

- Financially secure – Probably the key reason clients choose larger firms is confidence in the firm's long-term viability. Clients take a leap of faith when choosing to align with a service provider, and there's a greater sense of comfort when working with a 100-person firm than a five-person firm. That's a difficult objection to overcome, but not impossible. For years Avis successfully bragged about "trying harder" than its larger competitor, implying that it would work hard to earn your business and to keep it. The same approach can work successfully for smaller firms in any industry. And while you never want to appear that you need the work, there's nothing wrong with demonstrating how much you want the work—not by bearing gifts of tacky trinkets, but by doing your homework beforehand. An upfront investment of time and intellectual capital can effectively demonstrate your professional worth and push aside concerns of financial worth.

While it would be hyperbole to suggest that small is the new big, there can be no argument that size is a non-factor in delivering a quality product or service. What matters is how effectively you utilize the resources at your disposal. And if clients perceive that you deliver big value, they'll view your smallness as a serendipitous perk.

ROE #31

SPEAK GREEK ONLY IN GREECE

David Ogilvy, perhaps the greatest advertising mind of all time, stated that, "If you're trying to persuade people to do something or buy something, it seems to me you should use their language." It sounds so simple and logical, but most experts in a given field find it almost impossible to speak with the appropriate language and at the appropriate depth to make themselves readily understood by the layman. In their fascinating book, *Made to Stick*, the brothers Heath refer to this as the "Curse of Knowledge." Experts love what they do and find it hard to imagine that everyone does not share their passion and depth of knowledge. In short, they know too much for their own good.

Jargon is the primary culprit, and it's hard not to fall victim to its allure. Jargon demonstrates that we belong to a select group and possess specialized knowledge. It feeds our insatiable appetite to be part of a community and builds our self-esteem. It can also serve as a type of shorthand between experts in a given field. On the flipside, too many people hide behind jargon. They use it as a crutch.

It allows people to make believe they know more than they actually do, and to believe that they sound smarter than they actually are. Jargon is the linguistic equivalent of cosmetic surgery—it works on the surface but at the core it's the same old wrinkly same old.

Jargon is also presumptuous. It moves the conversation too far ahead. Clients need a context, while jargon assumes that the context is already known and understood. Without that context, clients are apt to nod their heads politely throughout a meeting or conversation, rather than asking questions that might make them look stupid. Then, after you've left, they'll shake their heads, wonder what you were talking about, and take a closer look at the competition.

Presumption is the driving force behind most communication problems with clients, and it goes far deeper than simply the use of jargon. Americans as a group think very highly of themselves, and we assume that everyone wants to be like us. Instead of celebrating the social and cultural differences that enrich our lives, we often try to eliminate them or pretend they don't exist. We expect a home court advantage regardless of where we are or whom we're with.

I distinctly remember the first time I traveled to Paris. Prior to leaving, I received multiple warnings that Parisians were rude and uniformly hated Americans. I was prepared for the worst but, to my delight, experienced the exact opposite. I found Parisians—as well as their compatriots residing in the beautiful French countryside—to be warm and friendly. Now I can't speak for my fellow American tourists, but I never entered a Paris café and expected the wait staff to speak English. I didn't speak English SLOWLY and LOUDLY to help these crazy foreigners understand me. Instead, I had my little translation dictionary and two years of high school French, and I made an effort. And the effort was clearly appreciated based on the excellent service and cordial treatment we were afforded.

Successful rainmakers make a similar effort to speak and understand their clients' language. That doesn't mean that a New Yorker should feign a Texas twang when meeting with southern clients, but he could certainly slow his speaking cadence, leave the Armani suit at home, and order iced tea at lunch rather than a decaf mocha cappuccino. These are little things that can make a big difference in how you're perceived and how you feel about yourself.

It's an interesting irony that language, which is designed to provide clarity and understanding between people, is often the means to deceive and delude. Obfuscation—a twenty-five dollar word that refers to the act of making something unnecessarily complicated—is especially prevalent in written documents. In an attempt to sound professional and official, we often use words and meandering sentence structures in writing that we would never use in spoken conversations. This happens despite the widespread knowledge that shorter words in shorter sentences have far greater impact and recall.

Of all the professions, law is the most frequent abuser of the English language. There's even a word for this abuse: legalese. It's gotten to the point that the state of California translated its traditional jury instructions into plain English. Here are two telling examples:

Before	After
A preponderance of the evidence.	More likely than not.
Circumstantial evidence is evidence that, if found to be true, proves a fact from which an inference of the existence of another fact may be drawn. A factual inference is a deduction that may logically and reasonably be drawn from one or more facts established by the evidence.	Some evidence proves a fact directly, such as testimony of a witness who saw a jet plane flying across the sky. Some evidence proves a fact indirectly, such as testimony of a witness who saw only the white trail that jet planes often leave. This indirect evidence is sometimes referred to as "circumstantial evidence." In either instance, the witness's testimony is evidence that a jet plane flew across the sky.

Regardless of your industry, it would be a valuable exercise to follow California's lead and take a fresh look at your suite of client communications and see how they can be improved. Identify what each communication is designed to accomplish and grade yourself on how well it achieves that goal. Use a highlighter to isolate those words that wouldn't be understood by the average fifth-grader. Force yourself to eliminate compound sentences and subordinate clauses (assuming you remember what those are). Eliminate jargon-based generalities having to do with value-added services, synergistic approaches, and holistic perspectives. Determine whether the same communication would work in Boston, Birmingham, and Boise. Most importantly, read the communication aloud. Does it sound like you? Does it sound like what your firm stands for? Does it make you proud or do you flinch a bit?

With all due respect to the inventor of the wheel and the discoverer of fire, the development of human language was far and away the greatest advance of civilization. Let's use it wisely for our mutual benefit.

ROE #32

LISTEN TO BE HEARD

When it comes to rainmaker marketing, the most sensitive erogenous zone by far is the ear. Conversely, the most insensitive is the mouth. That means that if you really want to get intimate with your customers, you need to shut your mouth and open your ears. It also wouldn't hurt to realize that never, in the history of the world, has anyone ever been accused of "listening too much."

So you have to listen more. Sounds easy enough. The problem, of course, is that marketers are people—and, like all people, they prefer the sound of their own voice to anyone else's. They like to hear themselves talk (or, even more frequently, opine and pontificate) even at the risk of drowning out the voices—and ideas, suggestions, concerns, etc.—of their customers, prospects, and colleagues.

This talk-over approach to marketing has a wealth of historical precedent. Until recently, marketing was viewed as a monologue. It was something you did to your audience. You determined the message, the medium, and the time and place of delivery. You interrupted people at home, at work, and at play. No one was safe and there was nowhere to hide. Mass marketing was what it was all about, and consumer cries of *no mas* were universally ignored. In truth, a few pioneering souls did make an effort to customize the marketing message to appeal to a more narrowly defined subsection of the target market—but it was still done on the marketer's terms.

Today, historical precedent doesn't go as far as it used to. In a world that is increasingly defined by two-way interactive activities like websurfing, TiVo-style television viewing, and instant messaging from our cell phones, effective marketing requires a dialogue. Sometimes you talk, and sometimes you listen. But most importantly, when it is your turn to talk, you better be damn sure that your words reflect what you've heard. Customers don't communicate with you for their own good, they communicate for your own good (which, ideally, will make your company, product, or service that much better and, as a result, will indeed end up being good for the customer as well).

The best example I can provide regarding the importance of listening is one I experienced about twenty years ago. I was doing a search for an ad agency and invited half a dozen agencies to participate. Five of the agencies showed up in packs of three or four—a senior partner to let me know I was important, a shaggy-haired creative type to demonstrate that they were "with it," an account executive who had just joined the firm from a larger cross-town rival (to demonstrate that they were up-and-coming), and occasionally a media director who pretty much guaranteed that she would blow every ad rep in the country to get me the best possible insertion rates. And then they'd dump a pile of samples on the table and drone on for what seemed like two or three lifetimes about how they had helped this or that company accomplish one thing or another. (Even more ridiculously, one of them actually showed up with a cold-packed New England-style clambake dinner for my colleagues and me.)

And then Number Six showed up. He came alone. He pulled out a yellow legal pad and started asking questions. We talked for an hour or so, as he took copious notes, and then he asked if he could come back the next day. He arrived the next day with one colleague, a written recap of what he'd learned during our previous conversation, and several carefully chosen samples of work his agency had done for other clients.

Guess who won the account?

Now guess why?

The first five companies believed I was looking for a good advertising agency. As a result, they assumed I wanted to hear them talking about just how good they really were. They came into the meeting knowing what they wanted to say, and paid little attention to what they wanted to hear and learn. The sixth understood that I was looking for a business partner—someone who understood my vision and someone who wanted to work with me to make that vision a reality. I was not going to be simply another notch on his agency headboard. He wasn't looking for a meaningless one-night stand; he wanted a long-term relationship.

Perhaps the most interesting thing about this episode is that he realized all of this even before I did. And he did so because he listened *actively*. The italics are there for an important reason. It is not enough to feign listening in order to appear interested and engaged. You need to listen, internalize, and extrapolate. Listening half-heartedly while thinking about what you're going to say next is transparent, rude and, unfortunately, all too common.

Active listening has no predetermined agenda and involves far more than simply hearing your client's spoken words. It requires a concentrated effort to help the client discover his needs and concerns. You can accomplish this via:

- Active questioning – You're the expert. By asking relevant and probing questions, you can help the client cut through the clutter and uncover the deep-seated problems that prompted him to seek you out in the first place. You need to probe way beyond the facts of the matter and reveal (thereby understanding) the client's innermost thoughts, feelings, and values.

- Interpreting what is not being said – Every story has at least two sides. Your client is probably enamored by only one of them. By actively listening to voice inflections and observing body language, you should be able to sketch out the other side of the coin. Indeed, pioneering research conducted by Professor Albert Mehrabian of UCLA suggests that only 7 percent of the meaning of spoken communications is derived from the words that are used. Fully 38 percent of derived meaning is based on the way the words are spoken, and 55 percent comes from the speaker's facial expressions.

- Identifying what cannot be said – Clients and prospects will often purposely hold back information out of fear ("my boss will kill me if I tell you this"), embarrassment ("even I can't believe how stupid I was"), or a host of other human emotions. This is decidedly tricky and dangerous ground, but a tangential line of questioning can often lead to increased insight.

- Inferring why something is being said – In larger groups, there are often one or two participants who repeatedly ask tough questions or aggressively challenge the expert. In many cases, these individuals are trying to demonstrate how smart they are to you and/or to their colleagues. They may also be resentful of the fact that a so-called expert was brought in and are trying to knock you down a peg or two. The flip side of this is the people who lob softball questions and nod approvingly at every pearl of wisdom that you share. They comprise the classic brown-nose subculture and should typically be kept at arm's length. Whatever the specific circumstances, you need to work hard to read between the lines and remember that *why* is as important as *how* and *what*.

- Understanding the context – As an active listener, you're a key part of the communication between you and your client. The way you present yourself and interact with the client will greatly impact your effectiveness. Everything you say or do needs to be appropriate to the given situation and audience. A one-on-one meeting with a prospective client who needs legal help with an upcoming IPO would take a much different course than a meeting with an existing client whose firm is accused of backdating stock options. The tone and volume of your voice (warm, casual, non-judgmental), your own body language (nodding, smiling, gesturing), and the words you choose to use (or not use) will all contribute to the client's openness to your ideas and receptiveness to taking the relationship to the next level.

Active listening takes the first giant step towards creating a dialogue and a dialogue is the first step in building a relationship. That means this concept is especially important with prospects and newer clients. If you have a 30-minute meeting, let the client talk for the first twenty minutes—using active listening and active follow-up questioning to get to the core of the individual's needs, fears and/or objectives. Use the next five minutes to recap what you've heard, ensure that your understanding of the matter coincides with the client's, demonstrate true empathy, and substantiate your ability to help him achieve his goal. Use the last five minutes to bring it all together, introduce a highly personalized game plan, and agree on the next steps.

Keep in mind that when it does come your time to speak, your best clients will utilize some of the same active listening techniques described above—and they will base much of their go/no-go decision on what they hear, observe, and interpret.

Of all the Rules of Engagement, "Listen to be Heard" is probably the easiest to execute. You just have to do the math. You have two ears and one mouth, so you should listen twice as much as you talk. And as a result of listening to your clients, they will far more readily open their ears (as well as their hearts, minds, and wallets) to what you have to say.

ROE #33

SAY *NYET* TO NYUK!

The Three Stooges are the quintessential role models for the in-your-face school of interpersonal relationships. They're also the antithetical models for building successful client relationships. Nyuk, nyuk may sound funny on television, but in the real world that type of full-frontal assault will offend far more people than it will befriend. Face-time with clients is an essential ingredient of rainmaking marketing—but there's a huge difference between face-to-face communication and in-your-face confrontation. Indeed, it's the difference between selling and marketing.

Good marketing is very much like a living, breathing organism. And like all living creatures it requires space—personal space and physical space—to flourish. Good marketing provides that space. It is respectful, and it informs rather than intimidates. Old-school selling driven by canned scripts and hard closes is what gives sales a bad name. The Alec Baldwin character in the brilliantly written and acted *Glengarry Glen Ross* distilled selling down to a three-letter mnemonic: ABC. "Always Be Closing! Always Be Closing!" And if that wasn't enough to motivate the troops, he spat out this warning, "You close or you hit the bricks."

It's easy to dismiss Baldwin's character as a Hollywood stereotype; and while I agree that Baldwin's performance was purposely over-the-top, far too many sales professionals were trained with that same ABC mentality that defines selling as an Us vs. Them endeavor. Let me share a personal example that illustrates how ingrained the "always be closing" mindset can be. It occurred a couple of days after my father died. My dad drove a Ford Crown Victoria. The size of the car had always intimidated my mom and she felt she needed something smaller now that she was on her own. My dad had always owned Fords and I didn't want to break with tradition, so I decided on a Taurus. I visited the closest Ford dealer and asked to speak with a sales manager. I explained the situation. My father had just died; I needed a new Taurus for my mom; I wanted to trade in the Crown Vic; and I didn't want to haggle. The sales manager proceeded to tell me about some great deals they had on Thunderbirds and demo Crown Victorias. I re-explained the circumstances and said I just wanted a basic Taurus. He then asked for my driver's license and wanted me to test drive a couple of cars, including the high-performance Taurus SHO. I thanked him for his trouble and left. I went to another dealer and the first words out of the sales manager's mouth after I explained my situation was, "I'm very sorry for your loss and I'm sure I can help." He grabbed a binder of current inventory and pointed out two Taurus models that fit the bill. As we went through the binder, he asked a colleague to appraise the Crown Victoria. In less than ten minutes, the deal was done. And it was sealed with a handshake. The sales manager said, "I can see you're upset. We'll get the car ready to pick up tomorrow and we can do the paperwork then."

The two sales managers approached me—and perceived me—in two startlingly different ways. The first was hardwired to sell and couldn't get out of his own way. He saw me as a prospect and nothing more. He was so focused on closing the sale, and hiking his commission by selling a higher priced car, that he lost the easiest sale he was ever going to make. The second immediately understood the situation and reacted in a way to make the transaction go as quickly and smoothly as possible. He allowed himself to stop selling and start feeling. He saw me as an individual, a fellow human being. And, perhaps, he saw himself being in a similar situation someday and acted accordingly.

Most importantly, the second sales manager demonstrated respect and acknowledgement—key ingredients in rainmaker marketing. Rather than always trying to close the sale, rainmakers show respect to their clients by acknowledging that decisions do take time. And they demonstrate empathy by acknowledging that they would want to do the exact same thing—take time to double-check the numbers, revisit the various alternatives, and ensure buy-in from all affected parties. The final step is their reaffirmation that they are available to help in any way possible. Rainmakers don't sell; they build a foundation for strong relationships and mutually positive experiences.

Whether at work, at home, or at play, people rarely remember more than a tiny fraction of what you said or did. They never, however, forget the way you made them feel. Respect, empathy, acknowledgement and affirmation all contribute to a positive and memorable experience—far more so than the old-school focus on features and functionality. People want to feel good about the products and services they purchase, and it's the rainmaking marketer's job to help customers envision the benefit they'll experience as a result of their purchase. And, once again, that is best done by getting out of the client's face and into his or her life. That's what Maxwell House did.

Maxwell House coffee owns bragging rights to one of the oldest and most successful branding campaigns in advertising history. Their "Good to the last drop" slogan has a pure Americana feel to it and is instantly recognizable to tens of millions of coffee drinkers and non-coffee drinkers alike. Notwithstanding any of that, Maxwell House changed their slogan to focus more on the customer than the product. Their new slogan is "Make every day good to the last drop." While the addition of three words may seem innocuous, they are designed to resonate with a younger generation of product-jaded consumers. It's also no coincidence that Maxwell House made the change just as Starbucks began appearing on every street corner. The Starbucks phenomenon is not about the coffee itself, it's about the experience. Starbucks is viewed as an integral part of people's lives in a way that Lou's Coffee Shop never could be. Maxwell House hoped to accomplish that same type of experiential involvement by associating itself with an optimistic mindset that appreciates the small moments that make our lives special. And, hey, our coffee ain't bad either.

Whether you're marketing and selling cars, coffee, catheters, or CRM systems, you'd be wise to take a step back and get out of your customer's face. Stop screaming about product features and start insinuating your product into the customer's broader lifestyle or business operation. In most cases, it's a given that the customer needs what you're selling. What they need is a nudge to help them see how all the parts fit together.

So get rid of the nyuks, and the *nyets* will disappear as well.

ROE #34

LOVE'EM *OR* LEAVE'EM

How could a book focused on building lasting relationships even hint at the benefits of a love'em and leave'em approach? Shouldn't effective marketing, like love, be forever? The concept of charming customers into your boudoir and then abandoning them should be anathema to any self-respecting rainmaker. Unless you're in a truly transactional industry, one-night stands will kill your business. Your customers will feel misled and mistreated. They'll feel they were oversold, used, and discarded.

On the flip side, however, there are always going to be a certain number of customers who don't deserve your love, and you're better off letting them go to the competition. It's like dating. You've got to kiss a lot of jerks and poseurs before you find a soul mate. In fact, oftentimes it's the experience with jerks and poseurs that helps you recognize and appreciate your soul mate when he or she enters your life. It's the same way in business. You'll be a lot happier and live longer if you work with people you like and respect.

Because rainmaking businesses are all about relationships, it's no coincidence that nightmare dates and nightmare clients have a lot in common. Here's a sampling of client-types to avoid and/or fire:

- Commitment-Phobic – These are the folks who continually ask for more information and have to run everything "up the flagpole." They view every new assignment or contract as a life-changing and terror-inducing situation. What if it doesn't work? Will I get blamed? What if there's a better solution out there? Am I getting the best price? I've gotten this far without XYZ; why do I need it now? What's the harm in waiting? And so on and so on with no end in sight.

- Tease – These are the clients and prospects who appear too good to be true. They possess all the attributes you look for. They have the financial resources, they're polite and professional, they ask the right questions, and they give the right answers. They just won't close the deal. The worst of the tease-types will use you to gather as much information as possible and then share your knowledge with a lower cost competitor or use it to develop their own solution.

- Cling-Ons – These are the people who are looking for more than your professional expertise and counsel. They want a soothsayer, confidante, best friend, psychiatrist, marriage counselor, and minister. They believe they are entitled to call you at any time of the day or night and, because you're viewed as a "friend," are shocked when you charge for your time. The important thing to realize is that these types likely have similar cling-on relationships with other professional service advisors. When they call to say "I know you're my accountant but would it be okay if I ask a legal question," you can be sure they're also calling their attorney to ask financial questions.

- Two-fers – These are the people who eat dinner at four-thirty in order to get the two-for-one special—and then they still go Dutch. It's all about the cost to them. They'll negotiate the price upfront and then argue about the bill. They want something, or everything, for nothing and couldn't care less that you're trying to earn a living. There's not a loyal fiber in their bodies and they'll toss you aside for the first "better deal" that comes along.

- Momma's Boys and Daddy's Little Girls – These are the folks who believe you should be honored just to be in their presence. They've been pampered their entire lives and expect nothing less from you. They are quite enamored of themselves and, in reality, are not sure they even need you or your services. They honestly believe that, if they only had the time, they could do it just as well themselves. They will question every piece of advice you tender, regardless of how far outside their span of knowledge, and will sprinkle in references to people and firms they've worked with in the past who are implicitly far mightier than you. It's always about them and you couldn't possibly understand the depth of their character.

- Trophy – If the sight of a trophy wife or boy-toy makes you cringe, you may want to take a closer look at some of your larger "prestige" clients. As good as they may appear on your client list, they may not look so good on the bottom line. They probably cost a lot to service and maintain and may be straining your organization to keep up with their needs— potentially even lowering the amount of attention and quality of service you provide to other clients. Ironically, as impressive as they are on your client list, they may actually deter smaller prospects from approaching you for fear of being the proverbial small fish.

A good rule of thumb when deciding whether to love or leave a client is your honest response to some simple questions: Do you enjoy working with them? Would you refer them to friends or colleagues? Do you trust them? Does having them as a client enhance your overall business or detract from it? If you had it to do over again, knowing what you know today, would you still take them on as a client?

Answering these questions is a lot easier than taking action and actually cutting ties with an existing client or walking away from a prospect, but it goes with the rainmaker territory. You're a business builder, and anything or anyone that hinders your success needs to be avoided or eliminated.

Most rainmakers are married to their business. That commitment is what makes them so successful. It's also what makes adherence to the "Marry in haste, repent in leisure" adage so imperative when choosing which clients to work with and which to leave at the altar.

ON A MORE POSITIVE NOTE

I'm not really as grumpy as I sound. The majority of the people you and I work with are delightful. They have idiosyncrasies and eccentricities, but that's okay. So do we. The best way to avoid the nightmare clients described above is to focus on attracting clients who are closer to your ideal. If you're not sure how to define your ideal client, I'd suggest looking in the mirror.

Most of us prefer to work with people like ourselves. That may sound sexist, racist, ageist, and elitist, and but it's the truth. Think about grade school, high school, and college. The smart kids hung out together. The jocks ate lunch together, and the cool kids partied together. As the rock band Bowling for Soup stated in their 2007 single, "High School Never Ends," none of that changes just because you have a job in the real world.

Not convinced? Make a list of your five best clients (defining "best" however you prefer) and describe them in depth. It should not be surprising that their descriptions sound similar.

It makes sense. If the attribute you enjoy most about Client-A also describes Client-B, odds are Client-B will also be among your favorites. What may be surprising, however, and perhaps even disturbing, is how closely the description of your favorite clients applies to you as well.

There's nothing mysterious or creepy about it. It doesn't mean you won't work with people outside your social or economic circle, it simply acknowledges that we have a natural affinity for people like ourselves. Similarly, prospects have a natural affinity for people like them—so it's a win-win for both parties. Use that knowledge to your advantage as you build your client list.

ROE #35

GO THE EXTRA 18 INCHES

In days of yore, world-class service meant going the extra mile to satisfy your customers' needs. The reality of today's marketplace, however, is that every one of your competitors is already going that extra mile. Trying harder, in and of itself, is no longer a differentiating factor. It's a price of entry. It's a requisite of a playing field that is becoming ever more level and ever more demanding.

So how can you stand out and differentiate yourself from the slew of competitors who are feverishly racing each other to go the extra mile faster and cheaper? The *Marketing for Rainmakers,* way is to travel a much shorter distance — 18 inches.

Eighteen inches is the approximate distance between the head and the heart. It also represents the final—and most important—step in transforming a transaction into a quality relationship.

Think about the times in your life when you've truly been engaged—totally absorbed in doing, watching, hearing, or feeling something. It's a visceral experience like no other. Athletes call it being in the zone. The head shuts down and the heart takes over. Thinking stops and instinct leads the way. And because the heart is the most vital organ when it comes to engaging people—it's your heart as a marketer that must lead the way for your customers' hearts to follow.

So how do you make that 18-inch leap? How do you allow your head to hand off the marketing baton to your heart? Well the first step is to stop thinking and start feeling. Test your thinking-to-feeling ratio by answering these three questions:

- Does your company brochure or web site state that you're customer-centric because you think that's what prospects want to hear or because that's how you truly feel?

- Do you begin client meetings by chit-chatting about their families and vacation plans because you're genuinely interested or because it makes it appear that you're interested?

- Do you ever wonder why it is that people actually buy the crap you're selling?

I trust that the third question caught you by surprise and appears to be out of place. It shouldn't have and it isn't. Way too many marketers have way too little understanding of what their companies are truly selling. They truly don't know how or why customers make the decision to purchase their product. They presume it's because of brilliant advertising, superior product features, clearly understood benefits, price, convenience, location, or a thousand other relatively concrete explanations. And maybe it is. But more likely it's because of squishier—more *heartfelt*—factors like the fact that the person the customer talked to on the phone had a smile in her voice, the person they met with listened more than he talked, the sales literature they read told a story they could believe in or—when it all came together—they simply believed *in their heart* that they were doing something good for themselves, their families, or their own company.

Virtually any product or service can be transformed into a heartfelt experience. If you doubt that, consider Michelin's success. If ever there were a product that could be reduced to technical specifications and cost comparisons, it would be the tire industry. There is no prestige factor in choosing Pirelli over Toyo tires (other than to the most devoted gearheads). And dollar-for-dollar, you tend to get the same quality from every manufacturer. Michelin has set itself apart, however, by placing that adorable little baby inside a Michelin tire and reminding mom and dad to choose wisely "because so much is riding on your tires."

The financial services industry has been a long-time advocate of heart-focused marketing. Insurance salesmen remind the breadwinner of the family that "life insurance is for the living." MasterCard hit a heartstrings homerun with its "some things are priceless" series of television and print ads. And in 2007, AIG introduced a campaign that linked healthier lifestyles— exemplified as laughing along with children, singing with friends, and playing with dogs—to longer life spans and the related need for retirement income that can last thirty or more years. The consistent theme is that there is a larger "common good" out there that needs to be factored into what seem like simple dollars-and-cents transactions.

Similar opportunities abound for every service or industry. Architects, real estate brokers, and interior designers paint joyful images of family gatherings. Cosmetic surgeons, personal trainers, aesthecians, and Billy Crystal focus on the ancillary physical and mental benefits of "looking marvelous." Accountants and attorneys highlight intangibles like the peace of mind that accompanies adherence to complex rules and regulations. And systems consultants still remind indecisive purchasing managers that "no one ever got fired for buying IBM" (albeit often replacing IBM with the likes of Cisco, Intel, or Oracle).

All of these examples rely on an intuitive understanding of what customers are buying from you. Adapt them for your own situation and focus more on capturing "share of heart" rather than market share. Success in the former will lead naturally to the latter.

ON THE OTHER HAND

An interesting corollary to heartfelt marketing is that even in those situations where the purchase decision is based on an emotional tug most individuals will need to rationalize their decision via more substantive facts and figures. As a result you need to provide your customers with all the backup necessary to justify the purchase "in case anyone asks."

ROE #36

TARNISH THE GOLDEN RULE

I'm sure our forefathers meant well, but their advice to "Do unto others as you would have them do unto you" is perhaps the most presumptuous cliché of all time. It also represents one of the key stumbling blocks in the development and enhancement of effective rainmaking and marketing skills. When taken literally, the Golden Rule suffers from the center-of-the-universe syndrome that, unfortunately, afflicts most of us modern folk—whether consciously or subconsciously.

Of course, in their defense, the world of our forefathers was quite different from today. The Golden Rule was derived in a world where most people were indeed very much alike. People lived in homogenous communities and typically lived their whole lives within a few miles of where they were born. Because of their proximity—in terms of geography, experiences, and DNA—people tended to have the same basic needs, the same aspirations (or lack thereof), and the same measures of happiness and fulfillment.

Not so today. High-speed transportation and communication systems have changed the world. Even people who live next door to each other in suburban or rural areas tend to be highly diverse. The traditional family structure of two heterosexual parents with two kids has been replaced with a wide array of living arrangements and personal lifestyles: unmarried couples, single parents, gay partners with or without kids, empty nesters, and lots more. Even the seemingly well-defined designation of "single parent" can have multiple meanings: never married, divorced, or widowed; biological children or adopted children. What commonality could there possibly be between the mindset of a widowed 45-year-old mother of three teenagers, who has not worked outside the house for ten years or more, and the 32-year-old lesbian executive who has just adopted a baby from China?

There is no one exactly like you or me. So we can't presume that a client or prospect wants to be treated the way we would like to be treated. *We* don't matter to the client. The only thing that does matter is that they get what they want, when they want it, in the way they want, and at the price they want. Everything else is noise.

The realities of the modern world require that the Golden Rule be changed to something along the lines of "Do onto others as they want to have done onto themselves." This approach moves you away from the nonsensical one-size-fits-all mindset that undermines successful marketing and long-term relationship-building. On the other hand, this approach also requires a much deeper knowledge of what the client truly wants. Virtually all salespeople, marketers, and rainmakers talk about delighting the customer and exceeding customer expectations. Very few of them actually accomplish that, however, because they don't spend the time to understand what the customer is expecting. In the end, it's a lot easier to sell what you've got rather than learn what the customer wants and then respond accordingly.

The fundamental problem with the Golden Rule is that it's all about you—whereas effective marketing is all about the customer. The complicating factor, however, is that our customers are all different as well, so we can't assume that Customer A has the same needs, goals, and hot buttons as Customer B. In *Predatory Marketing*, Britt Beemer and Robert Shook point out that "no one ever sold anything to a composite." Nor can you have a relationship with a composite. The trick is to identify commonalities among your clients and prospects—which in most cases is the need for whatever you're selling—and apply nuances that reflect the customer's specific industry, position, temperament, personality, attitude, aptitude, and every other idiosyncratic trait or thought process that impacts how he or she feels about you, your product, or your service.

The good news is that it's not as hard as it sounds. Today's Golden Rule is as simple as doing the right thing at the right time for the right reason. A.G. Edwards, one of the largest financial services companies in the nation, has successfully used this approach for over 120 years, believing that "putting the interests of your customer first is just plain smart business." That is the ultimate bottom line, because if your client succeeds, you'll succeed. Win-win scenarios in life and business are relatively rare, and thus should be aggressively pursued and relished. Which, of course, is a Golden Rule onto itself.

THE GOOD PARTS OF THE GOLDEN RULE

Notwithstanding any of this, the traditional Golden Rule does have relevance for rainmakers—most of which relates to common business courtesies like saying please and thank-you. Returning phone calls immediately. Treating all shared information— whether personal or professional—as confidential. Remembering names and using them at the beginning and end of all meetings and conversations. Not overusing names in a feeble effort to inspire rapport. Listening intently with ears, eyes, hands, face, head, heart, and every other part of the body that can communicate interest and respect. Not interrupting someone who's speaking. Pausing a moment when it is your turn to speak. Setting expectations upfront. Meeting budgets and deadlines. Communicating issues before they become crises. Avoiding shortcuts that shortchange you or the client. Being positive and enthusiastic with others even if you've had a bad day at home or the office. Focusing on expressing rather than impressing. And, most importantly, follow the lead of John Wesley, the eighteenth-century theologian, who advises:

> *"Do all the good you can,*
>
> *By all the means you can,*
>
> *In all the ways you can,*
>
> *In all the places you can,*
>
> *At all the times you can,*
>
> *To all the people you can,*
>
> *As long as ever you can."*

Section Five

The Competitive Rainmaking Marketer

ROE #37

SEE THE WHITES OF THEIR EYES

On September 1, 2007, the Appalachian State Mountaineers football team beat the Michigan Wolverines 34–32. Michigan had been ranked fifth in the preseason polls and was heavily favored to beat its Division 1-AA opponent. In fact, a Division 1-AA team had never beaten a ranked Division 1-A team. On paper it looked like no contest—a typical patsy being set up for slaughter by the Goliath who wanted a low-key tune-up game before diving into the heart of their schedule. Man-for-man, Appalachian State was clearly outmatched. Plus, Michigan had the home field advantage. Notwithstanding any of this, the game still had to be played; and when it was over, the underdog prevailed in what was immediately cited as the biggest upset in the history of college football. In retrospect it's apparent that Appalachian State benefited from a better game plan and better execution. But I would argue that Appalachian State also did a better job of studying, analyzing, and understanding the competition. Michigan, on the other hand, was focused on a Big 10 championship and a January bowl appearance. They weren't just looking beyond Appalachian State, they were looking through them as though they didn't even exist. Their competitive perspective was narrow and flawed.

Don't let that happen to you. Don't be one of those arrogant fools who believe that you needn't worry about your competitors because it's your job to make them worry about you. It's critically important to know and understand your competition. You need to watch them closely because they're watching your customers; and your customers, no matter how loyal and satisfied, are watching them as well. Perhaps most importantly, the competition helps establish and define customer expectations—expectations you have to acknowledge and respond to.

Many professional service providers will pooh-pooh all of this. They tend to believe that they don't have any direct competitors and that the very concept of competition is irrelevant in gentlemanly fields like law, architecture, engineering, and other advanced-degree professions. Let's consider these pitifully mistaken beliefs.

First off, everyone in every field has competition. If there's no competition, there's no real need for the product or service. People believe this falsehood because they view the competitive landscape too narrowly. Consider the Segway, the truly revolutionary gyroscopic "personal transporter" that debuted in December of 2001 and remains the only device of its kind. If ever there were a product that appeared to have no competition, it would be the Segway. There is literally nothing else like it on the market. But that doesn't matter; the Segway has a large number and a wide variety of competitors. It competes with automobiles, bicycles, scooters, Heelys (those cool sneakers with wheels embedded in the sole that I'm too old to wear), rollerblades, buses, trains, subways, and plain old walking shoes.

People need to get from one place to another, and the Segway is but one choice among many. Taking it a step further, the Segway can be considered a luxury-priced gadget and thus competes with gold-encased cell phones, massage chairs, hyperbaric chambers, and espresso-cappuccino machines for a share of the gadget-connoisseur's wallet.

The customer defines the competition. And because customers have a broad perspective of the world, we need to broaden our viewpoint as well. For example, medical doctors don't just compete with each other, they also compete with chiropractors, acupuncturists, WebMD.com, the pharmaceutical companies, naturopaths, and *Prevention* magazine. Graphic designers compete with do-it-yourself software like PrintShop and iPages. And architects compete with modular home builders. Customers have specific needs and they have many options to satisfy those needs. Whether you run a fitness club, provide tax-preparation services or consult on commercial real estate transactions, you ignore that reality at your own peril.

The corollary belief that competition doesn't really exist for the more "professional" professions stems from the widespread disdain with which most service providers view selling. Competition implies that there is an inherent pressure to sell. Being competitive somehow implies that you have to badmouth your competitors. And having a competitive spirit implies power-hungry greed. It's quite odd. Competition makes us try harder and become stronger. It does not mandate that we go for the jugular whenever the opportunity strikes. To the contrary, a competitive environment provides an opportunity to observe our competitors, learn from them, and appreciate the strengths, skills, and value they deliver to their clients. Competition need not be cutthroat and, because of the mutual benefits, is usually quite congenial. A lack of competition, on the other hand, breeds professional stasis and bodes poorly for the practitioner and his or her firm.

While you focus on better understanding your competition, it's important to not fall into the traps that ensnare many sales and marketing folks. Here's what not to do:

- Don't bet the over/under – It's interesting that the two most common faults with competitive analyses are diametrically opposed. CEOs, marketers, product developers, and salespeople tend to alternately overestimate or underestimate their competition. They either assume that the competition knows exactly what they're doing, or they posture that the competition is clueless. Inevitably, the truth is somewhere in the middle. The key is to not count on your customer's faults to drive your own success, nor to base your own strategy on their potential successes.

- Don't trip on footsteps – As an offshoot of their tendency to overestimate the competition, many business people blindly follow in the footsteps of their competitors believing that they must know where they're going. While there are some benefits in being a fast-follower and allowing the competition to identify and legitimize new markets, you'll never take the lead. Mimicking the competition's strategy and offerings positions you as a perennial also-ran. The goal of rainmaker marketing is to establish an advantage in the marketplace by bettering the competition—not simply matching them.

- Don't fire the messenger – The best way to keep abreast of competitive developments is to bring the competition in-house. But rather than actually hiring a staffer from a competing firm, designate someone within your organization to take on the persona of your key competitor. It then becomes his or her job to think, act, and react like the competitor. This approach allows you to better gauge how products and services might be received in the marketplace and provides a valuable forum to poke holes into strategic and tactical initiatives. It's akin to what college and professional football teams do when they prepare for an upcoming game by having the practice squad impersonate the opposing team. And just as the defensive team takes it easy when tackling the impersonators, don't take it out on your inhouse impersonators if they expose the cracks in your professional game plan.

- Don't be mindless – An all-or-nothing competitive mindset is not the goal. Winning at any cost usually involves compromising one's value system. Rainmakers rightfully cherish their integrity and ethics and allow nothing to reflect poorly on their character and reputation. Your competitive approach must always be mindful of the larger picture and thus avoid cutting corners that might add revenue and profit in the short term but which could irreparably damage your brand in the long run.

- Don't get personal – Fans of *The Godfather* movies will remember hearing several variations of the Mafia's "it's not personal, it's business" approach to their life's work. Despite my Sicilian ancestry, I only rarely endorse Mafia-like techniques. Nonetheless, I believe strongly in the value of keeping your personal beliefs and feelings separate from your business life. Emotions can and will cloud your judgment, especially when it relates to real or imagined competitors. I once worked with a family-owned business that seemed to take more enjoyment in beating down a particular competitor, who had once slighted them, than in building their own business. Competition is good; obsession is bad.

ROE #38

SHOP TILL YOU DROP

Tammy Faye Bakker said, "Shopping is cheaper than a psychiatrist." From the rainmaker's perspective, shopping is cheaper and more valuable than an MBA. Regardless of their business or industry, rainmaking marketers need to continually comparison shop with competitors—and do it with open eyes and an open mind. See what you can learn. Determine what your competitors do well and do it better. Find out what they're not so good at and avoid the same traps. This hands-on experience delivers the best variety of competitive research—empirical and qualitative rather than inferred and quantitative.

Shopping the competition gets you closer to the customers you most need to know—the ones that have chosen to work with another firm. While it sounds logical to assume that your competition's customers are just like yours, it would be presumptively foolish. If their customers truly were the same as yours, why wouldn't they be working with you? Unless we're talking about significant price differences or geographic distances, there have to be one or more specific reasons why they chose Firm A over Firm B. Up-close observation and interaction will help provide insights and answers. You might, for example, find that your competitor down the street attracts more female customers, has a younger, more affluent, or more educated clientele, or has a preponderance of healthcare workers, educators, or municipal employees. This type of observation indicates what's different about your respective customer base but doesn't yet get at why the difference exists. Perhaps the competitor has a large female following because the client-facing staff is predominantly female. Or maybe the competitor is active in women's affinity groups, aggressively markets in female-oriented media or, at the risk of sounding sexist, has created an enterprise-wide milieu that appeals to women. Likewise, the competitor may attract healthcare workers because the rainmaker has work experience or specialized knowledge in that field. And while it is highly unlikely that you could uproot the competitor's inroads with healthcare workers, that simple observation may lead you to target an affinity group with whom you share work experience and specialized knowledge. Keep in mind that it's not rocket science when rocket scientists are talking to other rocket scientists, but it is comforting to both parties to speak a common language. With what parties do you share a common language?

Just as customers are not customers, it's wrong to assume that accountants are accountants, and law firms are law firms. That's like saying that fast food is fast food. One visit each to McDonald's, Panera Bread, Subway, and Chipotle will convince you otherwise. Each of those establishments has a different vibe driven by the parent company's brand positioning and target market. Even at the local level, despite the cookie-cutter aspect of franchises, a McDonald's outlet in an airport food court feels different from one in a suburban mall or one on the ground floor of a high-rise office building in a big city. Similarly, a corporate law firm will feel different from firms specializing in personal

liability, environmental law, or criminal litigation. And as with
fast food franchises, each law firm office will have its own unique
vibe—even when comparing firms with similar specialties. Not
only will their offices look and feel different, their marketing
literature, web site, newsletters, and blogs will also have different
tones. Shop them all to compare your respective operations.

The "shop till you drop" ROE goes way beyond simply
experiencing and monitoring what your competition does. It
also includes all of your commerce-related experiences—medical
appointments, restaurant dining, retail purchases, hotel stays, car
servicing, tax preparation, home buying and remodeling, haircuts
and manicures, automobile rentals, personal banking and every
other activity that involves the exchange of money between two
parties. You can learn from every shopping experience if you tune
your mind to think that way. When I say that to people I often get
a lot of incredulous stares. How can I, they think to themselves,
learn something about lawyering/engineering/programming
from a retail clerk, service technician, or bank teller? Then I
tell them about my experience trying to buy a gift for my wife. I
approached the cosmetics counter of a *tres chic* department store
and was greeted by a lovely, young saleswoman wearing a crisp
white smock and a perfectly painted face that would have made
Renoir proud. She listened politely to my introductory stammer
and then started flinging questions at me regarding Laura's skin
type, color, tone, and complexion. I mentioned that Laura was
medium height and had blue eyes but that didn't seem to matter.
All I remember from then on was a litany of terms like lipids,
ceramides, botanicals and xerosis—all stated as interrogatories—
that I had never heard before and hoped to never hear again.
I ultimately determined that a gift certificate was the best bet
and quickly retreated. Later that night, when the cold shakes
subsided, I remember thinking that the cosmetic lady's world
wasn't too different from mine. When I spoke to clients about
their investment portfolios and tossed out terms like correlation,

standard deviation, and reversion to the mean, I often saw them enter the same trance-like state that had overcome me at the cosmetic counter. I wasn't just boring them, I was scaring the crap out of them. And rather than making me appear knowledgeable, I was making them feel stupid, inadequate, and, worst of all, unable to make a decision—just as the cosmetics lady had done to me.

It's quite easy to build a mindset that views every shopping experience as a learning opportunity. Just observe and ask yourself questions like these:

- How did the salesperson or cashier make you feel? Like you were an invited guest or an intruder? Like you were the first customer of the day or the last? Like you were an opportunity or an inconvenience? Like she recognized you or didn't even see you?

- What did the décor tell you about the firm itself and its target audience? Did it feel more like Wal-Mart or Target? Starbucks or Dunkin Donuts? An ER waiting room or a spa salon? A Four Seasons or a Marriott?

- Did you complete the transaction faster or slower than you had anticipated? Was the purchase decision simple or more complicated than necessary? Were you able to find what you wanted on your own or did you require assistance?

- Did you pay a fair price or feel ripped off? Did you settle for less than you had hoped for?

- Was the bill or invoice delivered promptly? Was it easy to understand and read? Was it accurate?

- Would you shop there again? Why or why not?

Keep in mind that your customers and competitors are doing this same type of comparison shopping—consciously or unconsciously—on a daily basis. You need to do it better and more effectively to keep your firm several paces ahead.

ROE #39

EXPERIENCE THE EXPERIENCE

In addition to experiencing your competitors' way of doing business, it's essential that you also experience your own business or practice. That experience, however, cannot happen in the home office via reports, conference calls, or PowerPoint presentations. Rather it depends exclusively on first-hand observation. The Japanese in general, and the Toyota Motor Corporation in particular, embrace a philosophy of *genchi genbutsu*, which translates to "go and see." There is nothing as powerful and insightful as firsthand experience and face-to-face interactions with clients and colleagues. And while *genchi genbutsu* may sound similar to more traditional business concepts like "management by wandering around," it involves a much deeper involvement and is focused solely on better understanding customers' wants, need, processes, procedures, and applications. Visiting clients with glad-hand extended may warm everyone's heart, but if it doesn't involve critical observation and learning then it's playacting that does little for the long-term benefit of your firm.

The concept of experiencing the experience comprises three equally important aspects—how your clients interact with your firm, your products, and you yourself.

HOW CLIENTS EXPERIENCE YOUR FIRM

Walt Disney used to regularly visit his theme parks, ride the attractions, and make detailed notes as to how the experience could be improved. Every quarter, Alfred Sloan of General Motors would leave the home office for a week and work in a dealership. And today, Amazon.com senior managers handle customer phone calls and email inquiries on a regular basis. The intent of all these examples is to put some meat behind the oft-quoted need to get closer to the customer. Whether you're a retailer, attorney, chiropractor, or graphic designer, you need to figure out how to do something similar and experience your firm the way your clients do. Here are some simple techniques to accomplish that:

- Shop – However possible, try to purchase your products and services the same way your customers would—through a sales rep, over the phone, in person, online, etc. For smaller firms and specialized professional services, this might require hiring a mystery shopper; but it would be money exceptionally well spent. Whether in person or on the phone, ask the sales rep some skill-testing questions to measure their knowledge level about product benefits, turnaround times, and the like.

- Visit – The more we see something the more blind we become to it. That applies especially to our workplace, and so the reception area, conference room, artwork, furniture, carpeting, and signage that we remember as classy and professional may exude a different vibe to clients. The best way to remove the blinders that we all wear is to slowly walk through your office with a video camera, zooming in and out to capture every angle and every detail. Play it back on a large television screen and do your best Ebert & Roeper thumbs-up and thumbs-down routine.

- Call – Recorded messages are often viewed as a must-have rather than an important marketing tool. Call your office number during off-hours and listen closely to the recorded message. Is it professional? Does it provide options in the event of an emergency? Is the voicemail system easy to navigate? Does the phone system play recorded music when clients are placed on hold? If so, is it appropriate and does it enhance or detract from your brand?

- Surf – The Internet has become an important tool for businesses of all types and sizes. And as much as people love surfing the web, they despise sites that are poorly designed, difficult to navigate, boring, uninformative, and static. Spend some time on your firm's web site and critically assess its pros and cons. Try to find a particular piece of information and see how many clicks it takes to get there. If the number is more than two, it's too many. Make sure you are utilizing the inherent power of the web—interactivity, dynamic content, and timeliness—to tell your story, attract prospects, and serve clients.

- Write – Despite living in a digital world, our professional lives still revolve around paperwork. We ask clients to complete applications, disclosure forms, business reply cards, surveys, and the like. Do something you've probably never done before and complete each of those forms yourself. If your firm is like most, you'll be horrified as you try to squeeze big words into tiny spaces or translate jargon-filled and stilted instructions into plain English.

HOW CLIENTS EXPERIENCE YOUR PRODUCTS

In addition to experiencing how customers interact with your firm, you need to understand how they use and benefit from your products and services. The anecdotal information provided by clients is a helpful starting point, but nothing beats spending time on client premises to see how they use your products in real time. One of the key insights you're likely to glean is that the value you place on certain product characteristics or the importance you place on one benefit over another may be quite different from the customer's perception. And that insight can help you enhance the product or service and further refine your marketing and sales positioning.

Clearly this works better for a product than it does with a service, but it is not impossible to gain insight on how professional services are used to benefit clients. Here are some examples to help you brainstorm how it might work for your particular industry:

- Attorneys, accountants, and consultants – contact clients a few months after an engagement is completed to check on how things worked out. Did the legal settlement solve all the issues or create new ones? Did the revised corporate structure create the tax savings envisioned? Have the actions items agreed on by management been acted upon?

- Graphic designers and web designers – check in with clients to measure the success of your contribution. Were response rates from the direct mail campaign higher or lower than expected?

How did the sales force respond to the new look? Have web usage and click-thru rates changed since the new design was introduced?

- Architects and interior designers – visit the homes of clients after they've lived with your design for several months. Ask what they would add, delete, or change in retrospect. What's their favorite room, piece of furniture, or design element? Is the answer to that question what they would have expected at the beginning of the project?

- Physical therapists and chiropractors – give clients a take-home "scorecard" on which to keep track of how well they're feeling using a 1-to-10 scale. Ask them to keep score daily for the first two weeks after their visit, and then weekly thereafter. Telephone them to gather their feedback or, better yet, build a simple interactive tool on your web site to track their progress in real time.

Relationships drive rainmaking success and, by definition, do not end when the sale is made or the project completed. Continual follow-up certainly serves to reinforce client relationships, but it delivers several other equally important benefits:

- Spending time with clients to understand how they use and benefit from your products sends a very powerful message to your staff and colleagues about your priorities and what you believe is critical to the success of your firm. As a rainmaker, you're an important role model and need to walk the talk.

- You learn what business you're truly in. It's a marketing cliché to say that people don't buy drills because they need a drill, but rather because they need a hole. By learning how clients use your products and services you can better understand their need—and craft even better solutions.

- You'll see your future through the eyes of your clients. Very few products and services are used in isolation, and seeing how they interact with other aspects of your customer's professional or personal life provides invaluable insight into product line enhancements and extensions.

How Clients Experience You

In marketing, as in all phases of life, there are three conflicting realities we deal with on a daily basis about ourselves (or our company):

1. The You as you see yourself

2. The You as you're seen by others

3. The You as you want to be seen by others

(Some would argue that there's a fourth reality—the *actual* You—but that gets into a whole philosophical digression that neither of us would enjoy, so let's stick with the three.)

The Johari Window, a psychological tool developed in 1955 and named for its inventors, Joseph Luft and Harry Ingham, provides a useful model to explore the interplay among our various interpersonal realities and gain insight into how we see ourselves versus how others see us.

The Johari Window

	Known to Self	Unknown to Self
Known to Others	OPEN My Public Self	BLIND My Blind Spots
Unknown to Others	HIDDEN My Hidden Self	UNKNOWN My Unconscious Self

The Johari Window distinguishes between what you know and don't know about yourself, and what others know or don't know about you. It then plots the overlaps, inconsistencies, and gaps into a four-paned "window" as depicted above. Each of the four window panes provides insight into a specific aspect of our communications and relationship-building behaviors:

- Open – This quadrant reflects your *public self*. Communication exchanges related to "open" topics are honest and straightforward with little defensiveness. As relationships progress this quadrant will grow larger, with the dividing lines moving downward or to the right. It's important to note, however, that some information in the Open pane may be information you would prefer to have remained hidden (e.g., a negative review of a new product or a report of declining growth). Nonetheless, because they represent public information, you have to be able to address them confidently and professionally.

- Blind – Think of this as the "spinach in the tooth" quadrant where all your blind spots congregate. Interpersonal communication in this pane tends to be hesitant and circumspect because others aren't quite sure what you know or don't know. Examples include a lack of eye contact when conversing, physical mannerisms like finger-tapping, and an arrogant tone of voice from someone who views himself as being "one of the people." Your goal is to make this pane the smallest of the quadrants.

- Hidden – If you have a skeleton in your closet, it lives here. To some extent, you control the flow of communication regarding information in this quadrant and share personal details only as circumstances and comfort levels dictate. In addition to secrets and embarrassing moments, examples may include personal belief systems such as religion and politics. As trust is built with others, a process of self-disclosure shrinks this pane as information migrates to the Open quadrant. Alternatively, hidden information that you would prefer to remain hidden may be revealed via extrapolation and observation.

- Unknown – This is the province of Freud and Jung where the unconscious reigns supreme. We don't know what we don't know and neither do the people we associate with. In terms of rainmaker marketing and relationship-building, this quadrant has limited application.

I doubt that Lily Tomlin was referring to the Johari Window when she said, "I always wanted to be somebody, but I should have been more specific," but her remark speaks to the primary benefit of the self-assessment tool. The Johari Window provides an opportunity to better align the realities, perceptions, and aspirations of your professional self—and better experience yourself as your clients do.

As a self-actualization tool, the Johari Window is relatively easy to use. There are several web sites that offer interactive tools to compile feedback from friends, colleagues, and clients to build your own Johari Window—and move one step closer to recognizing and understanding the *actual* You.

ROE #40

CHOOSE TO LOSE

The 14th century French philosopher Jean Buridan created a paradoxical analogy to illustrate the perils of choice. He told the story of an ass standing between two bales of hay of equal size and composition. Unable to decide which bale to eat first, the ass starved to death. Aristotle tells a similar story about a man, weakened by hunger and thirst, who is situated midway between food and water. Paralyzed by the deep-seated human instinct to choose the greater good, the man unduly prolongs his suffering as he fully evaluates the various options and outcomes. And Baruch Spinoza argues that man, faced with two equally appealing choices, cannot make a fully rational decision.

What's amazing is that all these guys were philosophizing long before the tall-venti-grande-chai-latte-mocha dilemma that we face every day at Starbucks.

So is choice inherently good or bad? The short answer is that some choice is good, but too much choice can be bad.

(Remember the *Seinfeld* episode about "good naked" and "bad naked"? It's kind of like that.)

The human psyche is a swirling combination of intellect and emotion, and most purchase decisions are based on the latter even if we consciously attribute them to the former. And since people are much more readily overwhelmed with emotion, rather than intellect, you can see where this is going.

As counterintuitive as it sounds, the surest way to lose customers is to give them too many choices. People are inundated with decision-making responsibilities. Think about your own life. Every single day you're faced with literally hundreds of personal and professional decisions. Take a walk through your local grocery store and if your choice of cereals, shampoos, sodas, detergents, and breads don't approach a thousand different options then you're living in the wrong neighborhood.

It didn't used to be that way. In the old days—back when I was a kid—there were essentially two choices for everything. Coffee was regular or decaf. Sneakers were designed for basketball or tennis. Television channels were UHF or VHF. Telephone service was provided by AT&T or you went without a phone.

It's a bit different today. We live in a culture of clutter. One good idea begets a hundred imitators. And who, for the most part, is to blame? People like me—professional marketers. We like choice. It makes our jobs more interesting. We can devise ever-more-granular Unique Selling Propositions and we can focus our marketing programs on increasingly narrow target markets.

But what's good for the marketing goose is not so good for the consuming gander. We've created an environment in which the experience of *buyer's remorse*—questioning whether you made the right purchase decision *after* the purchase has been made—is being replaced with *buyer's aversion*, a pre-purchase feeling of angst that leads directly to a paralysis-by-analysis mindset. If we make it too hard to choose, we make it very simple for the consumer to walk away. (Or even worse, we force the consumer into making a quick decision based on the one differentiating factor he actually understands: price. And that's a lose-lose proposition for anyone who doesn't happen to work for Wal-Mart.)

So what's the solution? It's fivefold:

First, and most obviously, you need to limit the amount of choice *you* offer (understanding full well that you cannot control the number of choices your competitors offer). Limiting choice, however, does not mean becoming dictatorial—my way or the highway. Rather it means spending more time to truly understand your audience and limiting the options you offer to those that will prove most desirable and beneficial to your clients. An upscale interior designer, for example, would possess a virtually limitless well of creativity. Nonetheless, when unveiling concepts to a client, she will typically present only two or three designs—having narrowed down the design choices based on input from the client and insight gathered from her years of experience.

Second, focus your efforts on helping your clients make informed decisions between choices that they can readily understand. Don't let them define their own criteria for selection. Instead, teach them how to choose. Demonstrate to them (which is much better than telling them) why your product or service is superior. Make sure they understand exactly why they need your product or service. An informed buyer is your best customer. She knows exactly what she's buying, how it's going to enhance her life, and why it's worth every penny she's paying.

Third, instill a belief in your clients that less is truly more when it comes to choice. You accomplish this by getting them to focus on what really matters and helping them to realize that everything else is extraneous. Once they start filtering out the noise, the purchase decision will be much easier, and customer retention and loyalty will be substantially enhanced. (Keep in mind that this won't work for everyone because there are people out there who actually enjoy the chaotic quest for perfection that can only be satisfied by an infinite number of choices. But that's okay, because these are the people who are least likely to be loyal long-term customers and who, for the most part, are not deserving of your time and attention.)

Fourth, present your clients with Yes/Yes choices rather than Yes/No choices. (Remember, it's not choice that's the problem; it's having too much choice.) Yes/Yes choices involve several (i.e., two or three) ways to access your products, services, and expertise. Yes/No choices force a decision between you and the competition.

And fifth, notwithstanding everything noted above, give the appearance of choice. In landmark research conducted by two Columbia University professors, supermarket shoppers encountered a tasting table offering samples of either six or twenty-four varieties of jams. The table displaying twenty-four different jams attracted 60 percent of passers-by, while the table with six jams enticed only 40 percent of shoppers to stop and have a taste. Despite the fact that the larger variety proved more desirable to shoppers at first glance, the multitude of choices proved to be a severely demotivating factor when it came to making a purchase decision. Of the shoppers who tasted at the table with twenty-four choices, only 3 percent actually purchased jam—versus a conversion rate of 30 percent among shoppers at the table with six choices. The lesson here is that it will pay to let clients know that you offer a wide array of services, as long as you pare them down to a manageable selection that is customized to meet the client's specific needs.

The bottom line is that profusion creates confusion. Limit choice and your clients will make their purchase decisions faster and simpler. The choice is yours.

ROE #41

ANALYZE THIS

Albert Szent-Gyorgyi, the Nobel prize-winning Hungarian biochemist, once defined research as "seeing what everyone else has seen and thinking what nobody else has thought." The brilliance of Szent-Gyorgi's statement derives from its clear understanding that facts and data points by themselves do not lead to breakthrough, rainmaker-caliber thinking. Rather it is the synthesis of hard data with softer experiential inputs—like personal observation, human psychology, and environmental factors—that results in true insight. Collecting and analyzing data does not automatically equate to market research. Data is quantitative, whereas true market research is highly qualitative. Data provides the foundation, but synthesis provides the springboard.

Data-centric market research is fundamentally limited because it can only measure or otherwise refer to what already exists. The vast majority of people can only dream and visualize in the context of what they have personally experienced. Most people truly do not know what they want. Henry Ford recognized this human shortcoming with a typically pithy observation: "If I had asked people what they wanted, they would have asked for a faster horse." Similarly, if Howard Schultz, the architect of the Starbucks brand, had asked people if they would travel out of their way, stand in line, and pay upwards of three dollars for a coffee, he would have torn up his business plan and begun considering alternative business models.

Asking people for their opinions is the weak link of market research. When answering questions, people typically provide one of two types of answers: the answer they believe the questioner wants to hear, or the answer that makes themselves sound smarter, hipper, more worldly, and/or more sophisticated. The problem is worsened when people are gathered together in focus groups. In addition to wanting to sound intelligent and provide the *correct* responses, focus group members want to please their cohorts. They want to fit in and, as a result, have a greatly increased susceptibility to groupthink. Even more problematically, focus groups are inherently flawed in their methodology. They create an artificial environment and then ask participants to intellectualize about product features and benefits—despite the fact that most purchase decisions are based on emotion rather than intellect. Suffice it to say that the McDonalds' McLean sandwich disaster was born of focus groups.

Direct observation is a far better market research tool than posing questions at focus groups. Going back to Howard Schultz, Starbucks can trace its origins to the cafes of Paris and Milan. During travels abroad, Schultz became enamored of European sensibilities when it came to food and drink. Cafes functioned as gathering places where coffee and pastries were celebrated rather than being slurped and hurriedly swallowed. Schultz believed that Americans would similarly be attracted to a quality social experience—even if it did cost more than having a Styrofoam cupful of watery brown liquid served by a bored, and frequently surly, convenience store clerk. Schultz didn't ask. He observed and he acted.

Without realizing it, Schultz was following the advice of John Scully, former president of Pepsi-Cola and CEO of Apple Computer, who was a strong advocate of not allowing the facts to get in the way of greatness. I'm not sure if Scully was referring to the New Coke debacle when he said, "No great marketing decisions have ever been made on quantitative data," but he does get at the core principle of the "Analyze This" ROE—marketing is much more of an art than a science. Too many marketers, however, try to hide behind statements like "the research shows" to lend some scientific credibility to their positions and thereby insulate themselves from accountability. Indeed, more often than not, research seems to be undertaken to confirm what the marketer already believes to be true. The mathematical underpinnings of "hard data" provide comfort to professional equivocators and serve as a personal safety net when things go awry.

Rainmaking marketers take a decidedly different approach to market research. They are less concerned about covering their derrieres and more concerned about uncovering the truths of the marketplace. Here's how they do it:

- They have a method to their madness – If you must ask questions as part of your market research, make sure the questions are relevant. As a lifelong marketer I've often been astounded, and occasionally horrified, at the questions asked by market researchers. The bottom line is that you should never ask a question unless the response will provide useful information. Whenever research results are presented and the consensus is that the information is "interesting," you can rest assured that it is also useless. Interesting information is like the ugly blind date with a nice personality and should be avoided at all costs.

- They test themselves before conducting research on others – This simple step would avoid much of the English-as-a-second-language lunacy that pervades most surveys and questionnaires. My favorite example in this regard comes from a large publicly traded financial services firm that attempts to determine the investment temperament of clients by asking whether they "strongly agree," "agree," "disagree," or "strongly disagree" with this statement: "My preferred investment would provide a high return over the long-term with low risk." Perhaps the company's investment returns are so bad that they're looking for people who enjoy getting low returns with high risk.

- They know when enough is enough – There reaches a point in every endeavor where you have to make a decision. This is especially true when it comes to market research. You can't fall in love with the data. Research is not an end unto itself, and over reliance on research data can lead to paralysis by analysis. So pick your spots and stop collecting data long before you've exhausted the evidence and exhausted yourself.

- They're comfortable with imprecision – Market research is rarely precise in its findings and often results in mixed messages and a lack of clarity. Waiting for perfection is a loser's game. In the end, market research gets thrown into the mixing bowl and takes on the flavor of all the other ingredients of running a business—from sales trends and brand perception to competitive pressures and product timetables.

- They sometimes ignore their clients – Nary a company exists that doesn't proclaim itself to be customer-centric. But as noble a calling as customer-centricity is, you need to have enough confidence in yourself to disregard a lot of what customers say for all of the reasons described earlier in this chapter.

- They pounce – Market research should accelerate the decision-making process not impede it. In our fast-moving world, research gets stale very quickly; and any advantage we might gain from insight into customer wants and needs will diminish if we allow it to percolate throughout the organization. The best time to smell the coffee is when it's just been brewed.

ROE #42

EXPECT THE UNEXPECTED

Field Marshall Helmuth von Moltke, Prussia's great military strategist, said, "No battle plan survives contact with the enemy." His core belief was that only the beginning stage of a military battle could truly be planned. Everything else consisted of an intricate system of options, variables, and contingencies. Preparation for war needed to consider every possible outcome and prepare for multiple what-if scenarios.

The same can be said for marketing. Notwithstanding the hobgoblin ROE, there are no absolutes in the world of marketing. It's important to be consistent, but inflexibility is a death wish. Markets and trends are changing at warp speeds and nothing is black-and-white. If it were, everyone would interpret the same data the same way, see the same trends, and react the same way.

As the bumper sticker says, "Shift Happens." In our world of constant change, marketing can be fraught with frustration. Product introductions are delayed or cancelled, budgets are cut, markets are entered or exited. Through it all, marketers need to remember that their strategic plans are a roadmap not a destination onto themselves. Any desire for (or obsession with) control demonstrates a failure to appreciate the power and wonder that spontaneity brings to the creative marketing process.

Twyla Tharp, the talented dancer and choreographer, wrote a wonderfully insightful book, *The Creative Habit: Learn It and Use It for Life,* that should be required reading for rainmakers in any line of work. Tharp adapts von Moltke's philosophy for the creative spirit: "The most productive artists I know have a plan in mind when they get down to work. They know what they want to accomplish, how to do it, and what to do if the process falls off track. But there's a fine line between good planning and overplanning. You never want the planning to inhibit the natural evolution of your work."

I like Tharp's perspective because, at its core, marketing is more art than science. Rainmaking marketing, in particular, relies on the free-flowing temperament of the artist to drive its success. If we move the analogy from dance to music, then rainmaking is more like jazz than a classical composition. It depends less on sticking to the score and following the conductor and involves more ad-libbing, jamming, reading the audience, and playing off their vibe. Rainmakers don't just accept and expect the unexpected, they thrive on it. Unexpected twists and turns to a business model or promotional campaign provide an opportunity for rainmaking marketers to utilize all their skills and gain the confidence to trust their gut. It's an invigorating experience that often leads to life- and/or career-changing epiphanies.

From a purely business standpoint, the practice of expecting the unexpected helps eliminate surprises—not totally, mind you—but in large part. Most companies have business continuity and disaster recovery plans in place that anticipate "surprise" fires, floods, hurricanes, electrical outages, sabotage, terrorism, and similar natural and systemic catastrophes. Following the advice of Aristotle who said, "It is likely that the unlikely will happen," modern businesses contemplate any and all horrific scenarios that might befall them. The emphasis, however, is almost always operational. Who will man the phones? Can the back-office functions relocate to another facility? What processes can be handled manually? How and for how long?

The smartest rainmakers adopt a similar approach to managing their business within a business. In the privacy of their offices, they adopt the persona of nervous Nellies and overprotective den mothers. As they should. Rainmaking marketers are stewards of the brand—their firm's and their own. Any event or circumstance that could damage the reputation or integrity of that brand is far more important than the operational inconveniences that accompany most natural disasters. The business continuity mindset of the rainmaker must paint the unexpected horizon with a very broad brush. Chance, by definition, cannot be controlled; and yet nothing can be left to chance. To wit, rainmaking marketers need to be prepared to deal with such unexpected events as:

- Economic downturns – e.g., the subprime mortgage meltdown of 2007 that, as of this writing, has pushed Countrywide Financial and Washington Mutual to the brink of bankruptcy

- Government regulations – e.g., the Eliot Spitzer and SEC probe on market-timing that damaged—and in some cases destroyed—venerable mutual fund companies like Strong Funds and Putnam Investments

- Deep-pocketed companies swooping in on "your turf" – e.g., the aggressive, and successful tactics of McDonald's and Dunkin' Donuts to capture mindshare and market share from Starbucks

- Dishonest employees – e.g., greed and funny-math stock manipulation a la Enron, WorldCom, and Tyco

- Stupid employees – e.g., Arthur Andersen's handling of the Enron debacle

- Psychosocial trends – e.g., the "green wave" that turned into a tsunami after the release of Al Gore's *An Inconvenient Truth*, and focused attention beyond gas-guzzling SUVs and fostered debate about such seemingly minor issues as the energy-usage differences between Plasma and LCD flat-screen televisions

- Landscape-changing innovation – e.g., the iPhone, FaceBook, and the Mini Cooper

It would be easy to dismiss these examples as part of the normal ebb and flow of commerce. They are *normal* events precisely because they happen, but they must also be viewed as *unexpected* because of the havoc they wreaked. Had they been expected, their impact could have been dramatically reduced. Indeed, had events of this sort been expected, the expectant firms could have reaped tremendous riches and kudos. So while Countrywide and Washington Mutual were left reeling, Goldman Sachs pocketed several billion dollars by anticipating the mortgage crisis. American Funds and Vanguard emerged from the SEC inquiries with reputations intact and won market share from their tainted counterparts. And Toyota earned praise from environmentalists for the hybrid Prius, while Detroit touted pickup trucks and SUVs with "25% better fuel economy" (conveniently ignoring the fact that moving from 12 mpg to 15 mpg was hardly praiseworthy).

So yes, the normal ebb and flow of business does include the unexpected. But it doesn't have to. Open your mind's eye to all the possibilities and visualize the iPod, Prius, or Wikipedia of your industry. Doing so will allow you to prepare for and moderate its impact or, if you are a rainmaker extraordinaire, you'll have the opportunity to co-opt the idea and introduce the innovation yourself—hoping your competitors were not quite as good at expecting the unexpected.

ROE #43

GIVE UP

It's scary. Professors J. Scott Armstrong of Wharton and Fred Collopy of Case Western conducted a study of MBA students and asked them whether the "primary purpose of the firm is (a) to do better than its competitors, or (b) to do the best it can." One-third of the students chose option "a," implying that beating the competition should take precedence over profitability, corporate integrity, customer satisfaction, and similar measures of business excellence. I suspect that a similar percentage of CEOs would make the same choice, in most cases for purely egotistical reasons.

I blame Jack Welch, the former CEO of General Electric. Welch fervently believed that GE would not and should not compete in any industry in which it could not be first or second in market share. While that strategy seems to have worked for Welch and GE during the 1980s and 1990s, the rest of the business world glommed onto this "truism" like frenzied lemmings rushing to be the first to drown. Welch created a corporate-think monster that turned people's attention away from the true prize—profitability.

In his book, *The Myth of Market Share*, Richard Miniter aptly describes market share as "the fool's gold of modern business." He points out that, seventy-five percent of the time, the most profitable company in a given industry is not the one with the largest market share. Rather, that distinction belongs to the company that rightfully views profitability as the primary goal. Increased market share may very well result from what you do as a business, but it should never be the driving force behind what you do as a business. Look no further than General Motors to see that market share is a poor barometer of corporate excellence.

In retrospect, I believe Jack Welch needs to share the blame with Sun Tzu, the ancient Chinese author of *The Art of War* and influencer of the rampant usage of military analogies and references in modern business. Far too many executives view business as war, with the marketplace as their battlefield. There is way too much talk about giving the troops more ammunition, adding another arrow to the salesman's quiver, getting down in the trenches, outflanking the enemy, and taking no prisoners. It's macho bravado at its worst, and it depletes time and money that could be better spent focused on the customer rather than the competition.

The multitalented financial journalist, James Surowiecki, provides an enlightening example of how even the smartest companies can get so caught up in a battle to win market share that they end up losers on multiple fronts. In his December 4, 2006 *New Yorker* article, "In Praise of Third Place," Surowiecki describes how Sony and Microsoft have battled fiercely in the video game market with their dueling PlayStation 3 and Xbox 360 systems. Sony and Microsoft have focused on leapfrogging each other by adding a steady stream of technological bells and whistles to their machines—turning them into multimedia interactive entertainment centers. But sometimes all people want is a good video game console—which is what Nintendo, the "laggard" in market share, delivered with its hugely popular Wii system. So despite being third in market share, Nintendo earned around a billion dollars in profit compared to Sony's break-even and Microsoft's money-losing performance. And it did so by ceding the presumably higher-end market to its larger rivals. By giving up that segment of the market, Nintendo was able to focus on its core competencies—and it's doubtful that any of its shareholders are complaining about low market share. Companies are in business to provide quality products that help (or in this case, entertain) people and earn a profit in the process. Accomplishing one without the other constitutes corporate failure. Nintendo understands that; Sony and Microsoft seem to struggle with the concept.

So what does this mean to all of us marketing-rainmaker types? In the simplest of words it means you sometimes have to give up something to get something. Business is not war. It's competitive for sure, but it's intelligently competitive. There is probably no activity on earth more competitive than the National Football League. (The more cosmopolitan of you will argue that World Cup soccer with its foaming-at-the-mouth fans is far more competitive than American football but, being a middle-aged American male who grew up playing real sports in which you're allowed to use your hands, I beg to differ and humbly accept the fact that you're grossly mistaken.) Anyway, even in professional football, teams will often "give up" short pass patterns to guard against the long bomb or even give up a two-point safety in order to worsen the opponent's field position.

Life and business are full of trade-offs. You've got to pick your spots carefully. Trying to succeed on all fronts (to use another lame military analogy—which should again remind you to do as I say not as I do) dooms your efforts. The marketplace is huge with plenty of room for you and your competitors. Spend less time worrying about their market share and more time figuring out how to deliver the best possible product and service. Market share doesn't tell you a whole lot about how well your company is really doing. Scant satisfaction can be derived from knowing you've got more customers than your chief competitor if those customers are not happy with your products, are not profitable, or are just one small price-cut away from taking their business to the competitor.

As you know by now, I am a big fan of Apple—both the company and the product line. Apple has long been a small player in the personal computer arena with a market share that hovered between one and two percent until its recent surge to a six or seven percent share. Over the years it's been dwarfed by the likes of Dell, IBM, HP, Compaq, Acer, Gateway, and Sony. It would have been very easy for Steve Jobs and company to introduce a less expensive Windows-based machine and capture significant market share due to Apple's strong brand awareness. But that was never an option. Apple long ago stopped paying attention to market share and instead focused on continuously improving its products and the customer's experience with those products. The company gave up competing with Dell and HP in order to stay true to Apple's mission—and to stay true to its legions of fans.

As a marketer and rainmaker, it is your responsibility to do the same for your company and your brand. Give up something small to gain something big.

Section Six

The Hardwired Rainmaking Marketer

ROE #44

Tell a Story Worth a Thousand Pictures

If you believe the adage that "a picture is worth a thousand words," then the logical conclusion of this chapter title is that a story is worth a million words. But if you've read this far in the book, you should realize that logic is highly overrated when it comes to successful rainmaking and best-in-class marketing.

The point is that the most powerful picture of all is a word-picture—more commonly referred to as a story.

Stories strike a powerful chord because they come from the heart. They're comfort food for the soul. They're dramatic and far more memorable than the typical marketing litany of facts and figures. Stories play into our hardwired need for connections. Parents read stories to their children. Couples fall in love—and stay in love—by sharing stories. And from the rainmaker's perspective, stories are the most effective way to engage your audience, build rapport, and create a strong foundation for a lifetime relationship.

In a sense, stories constitute a form of marketing shorthand. They make the unfamiliar sound familiar, and they paint a vivid picture in the customer's mind. When people read or hear a story, it has instant credibility because it provides a context. It creates relevancy. Stories make the audience relax and become more receptive to the underlying message. And because a story is usually an entity onto itself, it requires no further explanation. A well-crafted story is every marketer's dream—a self-contained, immediately impactful, interest-generating embodiment of all that your product or service has to offer.

It would not be an exaggeration to say that stories are the Holy Grail of marketing. Unfortunately they are equally elusive.

The irony is that most marketing materials already utilize a traditional storytelling structure. Like stories, most marketing materials have a beginning (the clever headline), a middle (the features and benefits), and an end (the call-to-action). The difference lies in the degree of engagement. Stories capture one's attention because they focus on relationships and provide emotional insights. Marketing materials, because they're so entwined with the sales process, have traditionally been focused on transactions—getting the client to purchase, rent, or lease whatever it is that you're selling. They typically suffer from information overload and rarely observe the world from the customer's point of view. Stories, on the other hand, cut through the clutter and share a common perspective with the audience.

Consider this somewhat offbeat example. A beggar is standing on a city sidewalk holding a sign that says, "I am blind." Think about how many people—including yourself—would slow down enough to absorb the full meaning of the man's plight, let alone toss a few coins his way. Now picture the exact same beggar standing alongside the Tidal Basin in Washington, D.C. This time his sign reads, "It's cherry blossom time and I am blind." It would not be a stretch to imagine that the second approach would attract exponentially higher contributions than the first.

The beggar's trick was to get his prospects (i.e., passersby) emotionally involved by telling them a story. A story that went far beyond the facts and communicated at a visceral level.

The moral of the story is this. The first beggar was selling; the second was marketing.

So how do you apply the lesson of the two beggars to your business? First off, don't fret about having to create a long and involved story. The second beggar told his story using only eight words. Anheuser-Busch, one of the greatest marketing machines in the world, tells a powerful story in even fewer words. Here's what they do. Instead of printing an expiration date on bottles and cans of Budweiser, they announce that the beer was "born on Month/Day/Year." So while virtually every other purveyor of food and drink provides an expiration date or a best-if-used-by date, Budweiser tells us how young their beer is rather than warning us of how old it can be before spoiling. That in itself is brilliant marketing, but it gets even better when you consider all the connotations of the born-on-date phraseology. Living, breathing organisms like puppies and kittens are born. Inanimate objects like fishing licenses, magazine subscriptions, and automobile registrations expire.

Budweiser transformed a simple fact into a powerful story. And perhaps most importantly, they built a story that no one else in their market space can co-opt without looking like a pathetically uncreative copycat. Budweiser got there first and staked their claim. They created a competitive advantage where none existed. And they did so, not by saying something new, but rather by saying something in a new and different manner—thereby eliciting a decidedly different and emotionally deeper response.

A classic example of a company that sees the same thing as its competitors but thinks about it in a different way comes from American Funds, one of the largest and most successful investment companies in the world.

American Funds has told the story of "Louie the Loser" for several decades. Louie's story is indeed a sad one. His desert vacations get rained out. He cancels his dental insurance just before he needs a root canal. He misses planes but catches colds. And he makes one $10,000 investment per year into a mutual fund. The bad news is that, somehow, each and every year, he manages to pick the worst possible day to invest—the day that the stock market hits its high for the year. The odd thing is that Louie is a very happy investor. Despite his terrible timing, over the years his investment portfolio enjoyed steady, double-digit growth. And he learned that even though the market has up days and down days—any day is a good day to invest.

Virtually every investment firm preaches the value of investing at regular intervals rather than trying to time the market, but most do it with tables, pie charts, and graphs. American Funds chose a more memorable approach—a simple story that most everyone can relate to and identify with.

As you think about creating a story for your own business, note that the stories told by the blind man, Budweiser, and American Funds share a key element: specificity. While facts and figures by themselves are cold and off-putting, they also serve as the backbone of stories. Indeed, stories would collapse under their own weight without a strong and relevant factual infrastructure. Perhaps the best way to think about all of this is to view facts as the skeleton and stories as the flesh. Facts provide the framework—cherry blossom time, a specific date, a character's name—while the contextual story infuses life. Consider how less engaging the American Funds story would be if Louie didn't have a name. Similarly, if the blind man had substituted "a warm April day" for "cherry blossom time" his story would have lost much of its impact.

Stories—being word pictures—show rather than tell. They help the audience visualize the benefits that the given product or service can deliver. That's why infomercials, testimonials, and case studies work so well. That's why spokespeople like the Maytag repair man, the GEICO caveman, and the bantering Mac and PC in Apple's "I'm a Mac" series are so effective. Your customers and prospects, being human, are social beings. They thrive on connections. Give them a story to connect with, and you'll thrive right alongside them.

ROE #45

French KISS

The KISS principle to "Keep it simple, stupid" is probably the most frequently given—but least frequently followed—piece of advice that marketers ever encounter. I suggest three reasons for this.

First off, it's difficult to keep things simple. It's hard to pare down 500 words of drivel into 200 carefully selected words that would make Shakespeare or his marketing counterpart, Ben Ogilvy, gasp with joy.

Secondly, obfuscation of any kind creates euphoric feelings of job security. After all, if sales and marketing folk make their jobs look too simple, the finance guys might suggest that fewer of them are needed or, worse yet, that they're grossly overpaid for what they do.

Third, being human and all, salesmen and marketers often equate simplicity with dullness.

The first two issues can be dismissed with three words—"get over it"—while the third provides the inspiration for the French KISS principle.

The French KISS—like its physical namesake—improves upon the original by adding some spice. It's not afraid to be a bit daring. It's comfortable exploring the nooks and crannies of your imagination. And like all good marketing efforts, it's customer-centric—totally focused on the target audience.

Of all the Rules of Engagement, it's the French KISS principle that had the greatest impact on shaping this book. And I believe my own encounter with French KISSing provides a perfect example of how to bring the principle to life. Here's what happened.

When I started writing the book, I made a list of simple ways rainmaking marketers could better connect with their customers. As strong as I believed the concept was, I knew something wasn't quite right. So I walked away from the project for a couple of days, and then reread the outline. Within seconds I realized that I had violated the core message that I was trying to communicate. The approach I was taking was not going to connect with or engage a single reader. I was writing a textbook which, while conversational in tone, was not going to engender the kind of internal dialogue that would serve as a catalyst to actually change one's behavior. The problem was that I was kissing with my lips clenched shut—an embarrassing predicament for me and a painful experience for you, the reader.

The root of the problem was the chapter titles—the names I had assigned to the 52 Rules of Engagement. They were short. They were descriptive. And they were certainly simple. They embodied every aspect of the KISS principle. Unfortunately, they were also impersonal and indifferent. So I changed them. ROE #1, which started out as "Focus," turned into "Begin at the End." ROE #2, which began life as "Consistency," transformed into "Be a Hobgoblin;" and ROE #46, which was titled "Integrity," became "Light Your Lying Pants on Fire."

So, with profuse apologies to *Casablanca*, the lesson I learned—and the lesson I share—is that "a KISS is just a KISS" but a French KISS goes a bit deeper, is visceral rather than rational, startles and invigorates, and truly serves as the beginning of a beautiful relationship.

HOW TO BECOME A BETTER FRENCH KISSER

I've never spoken to his wife, but I would have to say that Steve Jobs is the greatest French KISSer in the history of the world. There are countless reasons for this, but here are two of them:

- The iMac – While traditional PC manufacturers focused on making their computers easier to set up by color coding the connecting wires and ports so users could more readily distinguish between the assorted keyboard, mouse, monitor, and speaker connections, Apple introduced all-in-one computers that were brightly colored (the tangerine model was especially popular), pretty much set themselves up, and eliminated all but a few cords and cables. Apple made computers a fun and decorative accessory rather than a drab beige machine that you hid in the basement or darkened corner. The iMac was followed by the clamshell-shaped iBooks featuring similar bring-a-smile-to-your-face color palettes. Tangerine-colored or polka-dotted computers had to be easy to use—even if they didn't have color-coded cables.

- The iPod – Despite the ubiquity of the iPod, Apple did not invent MP3 players. In fact, they were rather late to the game when they introduced the iPod in October, 2001. Several other manufacturers, including Rio and Creative Arts, had been selling MP3 players for several years. What distinguished the iPod, and drove its success, was not the device itself (as beautifully designed as it was). Rather, the genius of the iPod was the "iProcess"—the way the device seamlessly and intuitively integrated with iTunes and the iTunes Store. Not only was playing your music easy, it was now unbelievably easy to add tracks from your favorite CDs, organize them into self-selected categories, and buy songs from current and backlist artists—without having to buy the whole album and without breaking Federal copyright laws. Sure, it was an idea whose time had come, but it was an idea that could have been acted upon by the likes of Sony, Time Warner, Hewlett-Packard, and countless other media, entertainment, and technology companies. But none of them had the vision of Steve Jobs.

So how can the example of Steve Jobs help you attract and retain clients with your own French KISSes? By focusing on the entire experience. Rather than limiting his vision to functional simplicity, Jobs pursued holistic simplicity. Color-coded cables don't translate into a true KISS encounter if the rest of the computing experience is a train wreck. That's where most marketers drop the ball. They overconcentrate on simplifying a single aspect of the customer experience—typically at or near the beginning of the client-vendor relationship. They focus on making the purchase decision easy and friendly—no paperwork, free consultation, personal attention—and then, once the customer has committed, they move on to the next prospect, leaving the once-courted client feeling used and abused. A true French KISS must be a total body experience—from start to finish—with no end in sight.

The French KISS principle can also be applied to bringing your value proposition to life and making it more memorable. Think about how many times you've heard companies talk about ease-of-use or how often you've heard the expression "so easy a child could do it." Empty promises (particularly of the non-specific variety) and unimaginative analogies or metaphors do nothing to enhance your brand. But consider what happens when you add a simple twist, as GEICO did with their "so easy a caveman can do it." You can then own that unique positioning in the minds of clients and prospects.

Here's another example of the French KISS principle in action. Staples, the big-box office supply chain, condensed their entire value proposition into three words: "that was easy." They supported it with their innovative "Easy Rebate" program, introduced a simplified ink-jet cartridge recycling program, and enhanced their loyalty rewards program. Their three word French KISS proved so compelling to customers that Staples actually manufactured and packaged the "Easy Button," gave it a prime impulse-buying position near the checkout counters, and sold over 1.5 million units through the end of 2006 (and, in the process, donated $2 million of the proceeds to the Boys and Girls Clubs of America). In one fell swoop Staples solidified its position in a highly competitive industry, rallied its employees around a simple theme, created an army of customer-apostles to spread the Staples message, and contributed to society at-large. And that, my friends, is a holistically inspired French KISS by any standard of measure.

WARNING: DO NOT TRY THIS AT HOME

French KISSing takes practice. A lot of practice. And you should really focus on becoming adept at KISSing before you start tossing slobbery French KISSes all over the place. Apple computers were easy to use even before the multicolored iMacs were introduced. And Staples had a long-standing reputation for a hassle-free shopping experience.

You also need to choose your spots. French KISSes are not always appropriate. Indeed, sometimes regular, old-fashioned, closed-mouth KISSes are all you need to close the deal. An Easy Button would not work particularly well for a divorce lawyer or cosmetic surgeon—whereas KISS stalwarts like plain English communications and simplified billing can pay big dividends.

Above all, don't forcibly make the leap from handshakes to French KISSes—or you may end up kissing in the wind.

ROE #46

LIGHT YOUR LYING PANTS ON FIRE

Someone once said that, "Character is how we live our lives when no one else is around to notice." Character—whether defined as integrity, trustworthiness, honor, or reliability—is an essential ingredient of success at any endeavor. And that's especially true when it comes to the dynamic duo of rainmaking and marketing. Keep your promises, and you'll keep your customers.

So what's so hard about being trustworthy or about keeping promises? Well for many marketers and salespeople, it runs counter to everything they've been taught. Remember the "sell the sizzle" definition of marketing? Boiled down to its essence, sizzle is simply a euphemism for smoke-and-mirrors. It's all about erecting facades. It's like a shiny new paint job on a broken down jalopy—it may look good but it's not going to get you where you want to go.

Traditional marketing revolves around hyperbole. Never let the facts get in the way of a catchy tagline. Just capture the consumer's attention, lock him into a purchase decision, and wish for the best. It's an approach that works fine for a transactional relationship but bodes disaster for the kind of lifetime relationship that successful rainmaker marketing strives to create. It's the antithesis of the ROE dictum to under-promise and overdeliver. Good marketing does not employ sleight of hand. It doesn't attract prospects via rigged shell games.

Brand managers—whether in one-person shops or Fortune 500 companies—tend to focus on ensuring consistency in the look and feel of their logo. They spend far too much time worrying about fonts and pantone colors. Instead they should be worrying about the *character* of their brand. They should be focusing on how to turn their trademark into a registered "trustmark"—a brand that stands for uncompromised integrity. A brand that will never mislead, never disappoint and, most importantly, never take itself or its customers for granted.

Branding is ultimately about the promise made to the buyer. That promise could be based on product quality, service, or whatever—but it creates a bond of trust between the consumer and the product.

Consider the example of non-aspirin pain relievers—specifically those based on the active ingredient acetaminophen. There is one dominant brand in this category—Tylenol—and a host of generic competitors. Tylenol and its generic counterparts are identical in composition, using the same core ingredients and providing the exact same benefits. Tylenol, however, usually costs about twice as much as the generic version. Despite that cost differential, Tylenol outsells every generic competitor combined. What's really interesting about this, however, is that even those people who buy the generic version for their own use will still opt for Tylenol when they're buying it for a parent, child, spouse or other loved one. Why is that? Because people associate Tylenol with quality. They have confidence in the product. They trust the manufacturer, and they don't mind paying more for perceived quality. Most importantly, the purchase makes them feel good about themselves. Put it all together and it sounds a lot like why people choose one attorney/advisor/accountant/architect over another.

In all aspects of life and business, it's quite easy to bend the rules ever so slightly. And it seems harmless enough. A little exaggeration here or there can't hurt anyone. Plus, most people don't believe everything they read in a brochure or hear from a salesman anyway. Exaggeration is expected; it's all part of the game. In a word, that's nonsense.

When I was heading off to college, my father took me aside and gave me some sage advice: "It's easy to get into trouble, but hard to get out of it." That advice works for integrity as well. "It's easy to lose one's integrity, but very hard to earn it back." Friedrich Nietzsche, the nineteenth-century German philosopher, expressed the concept this way: "What upsets me is not that you lied to me, but that I can no longer believe you." There is no downside to the truth, and no upside to lies.

Successful rainmaking and marketing hinge on your character and integrity. If you truly love what you do and passionately believe in the products and services you offer, you won't be tempted to take the easy way out—and your exaggerated claims, hyperbolic verbiage, and little white lies will never come back to haunt you.

Make the Most of a Bad Situation

Unfortunately, bad stuff does tend to happen in life and business. So what happens if you do mislead or misrepresent—whether intentionally or not? What if something goes wrong somewhere in your company or its related supply chain that disappoints your clients or is viewed by them as a failure? As a rainmaker, and as the primary point of contact between your firm and the marketplace, customers will look to you for resolution and restitution. Most immediately, however, they will look to you for an acknowledgement of the problem and an apology. And it can't be one of those insincere apologies that our mothers forced us to mutter after beating up our little brother. A hollow apology will leave your reputation in tatters. A sincere apology will minimize damage to the relationship, buy time to fully resolve the problem, and create a Eureka moment for your clients when they say to themselves, "I can't think of any other person or company that would respond to this situation so quickly, so empathetically, and so professionally."

Southwest Airlines has such a strong belief in maintaining the trust of their customers that they created a position with the title of "Senior Manager of Proactive Customer Communications." This role, which is unofficially called the "Chief Apology Officer," is focused on identifying instances when Southwest disappointed its customers and then crafting personally written letters of apology. Whatever business you're in, implementing a similar approach could well represent the most important "C-level" activity in your organization.

MAKE THE CHOICE

H. Norman Schwarzkopf, the respected hero of Desert Storm (the "good" Iraqi war of 1990) remarked that, "Leadership is a potent combination of strategy and character. But if you must be without one, be without the strategy." Substitute "effective marketing" for "leadership" and the sentence reads just as true.

Be an incredibly credible marketer, and you'll be an incredibly successful marketer as well.

A FINAL NOTE

In the immortal words of that gravelly voiced troubadour, Tom Waits, "the large print giveth, the small print taketh away."

ROE #47

SELL SOFT, MARKET HARD

Way back in the introductory chapter, I defined marketing as the act of motivating someone to take action. Marketing means getting people to want to buy, whereas selling is a manipulative process to close the deal quickly so you can move on to the next prospect. Selling focuses on the transaction, whereas marketing focuses on building relationships that will result in a long-term series of transactions.

Rainmakers do not sell. Never. They create an environment and a multidimensional dialogue in which the client can visualize and experience the benefits of the particular product or service. Most importantly, rainmaker-style marketing is about proffering advice and helping to guide the client through his or her personal decision tree. And they accomplish this not by a series of self-serving statements, but rather by asking well-targeted and increasingly specific questions. Statements let people know what you're thinking; questions elicit what others are thinking.

I recently experienced a perfect example of how soft-selling and hard-marketing can make a big difference in both perception and reality. My business partner and I were looking for new office space. We wanted to move quickly and were willing to pay market rates. You would think that this presented a prime opportunity that real estate brokers would jump all over. The reality, however, was quite the opposite. Brokers did not return phone calls, could not answer the most basic questions regarding the properties they showed us, and disregarded the key features we were looking for. They didn't listen and they didn't seem to care. And then we found Jay Blacker of the Denenberg Realty Group. We had responded to a simple ad he had placed on CraigsList.com. The first time I called, he was about to step into a meeting and said he would call back within twenty minutes, which he did. He asked a few basic questions and asked if he could meet with us at our temporary office space. I knew immediately that Jay approached his career differently than the other brokers we had dealt with. No one else had even hinted of meeting with us prior to showing us properties. When Jay visited our office, he used it as an opportunity to better assess what we were looking for in terms of what we liked and didn't like about our current space. He asked questions to help gauge the relative importance of such variables as windowed offices vs. inside offices, our need for conference rooms and kitchens, lease duration, and parking availability. He wanted to know how often clients would visit and how large a reception area we would need. These all sound like commonsense questions, but none of Jay's competitors asked them. After his initial fact-finding, Jay explained how he worked with clients and gave us a list of references of local business owners he had helped. And rather than showing us just the one property we had inquired about, he suggested we schedule a block of time the following week to look at a half-dozen properties that fit our requirements so we could make side-by-side comparisons. When the day came, he prepped us with key information before we entered each space, and pointed out the pros and cons of each option as we toured the sites. He never tried to sway us towards one property over another; rather, he genuinely wanted us to find space that suited our needs. And we did, and Jay walked beside us through the proposal process and the leasing contract. He didn't close the sale; he facilitated the buy.

The last place you would ever expect to see soft-selling and hard-marketing is in retail. And that's especially true in regard to furniture stores. Most furniture stores are mom-and-pop regional operations, and they rely heavily on print and television ads that scream at the viewer and pretty much insult the intelligence of anyone over the age of eleven. Price would appear to be the key differentiator and "one-day sales," "massive markdowns," and "lowest prices of the season" are the norm. Except for Jordan's Furniture. Jordan's, which is now owned by Warren Buffet's Berkshire Hathaway holding company, traces its heritage back to 1918 and is still run by the grandsons of the founder. The Jordan brothers, Eliot and Barry, are the savviest marketers I've ever had the pleasure of observing as a consumer. They cast aside all the traditional approaches to furniture selling and created a phenomenon that sells more furniture per square foot than any other furniture retailer in the country. Jordan's never has a sale. Instead, they feature "under pricing"—the same low price every day—and offer a price match guarantee. The Jordan's sales team is knowledgeable and professional. They don't lie in wait to pounce as you enter the store. They offer assistance as- and when-needed. They are no-commission and no-pressure. What really distinguishes Jordan's is that they have accomplished the near impossible. They have turned their stores into destinations—family-oriented, themed destinations. It all started when Jordan's began staying open late on Saturday nights and promoting itself as a date-night destination. Furniture shopping didn't have to be an ordeal; it could be fun. Growing from that simple concept, Jordan's stores now feature IMAX theaters screening first-run movies, MOM (Motion Odyssey Movie) virtual roller coasters, themed restaurants, and huge reception areas (without a trace of furniture) modeled after New Orleans' Bourbon Street that feature music, lights, and special effects that delight young and old. Of all their innovative marketing campaigns, none was more brilliant than the "Monster Deal" they ran in the spring of 2007. Named after Fenway Park's "Green Monster" leftfield wall, Jordan's promised to refund the price of mattresses, dining tables, sofas, or beds purchased between March 7 and April 16 if the Red Sox won the World Series. The citizens of Red Sox Nation came out in full force and placed about 30,000 orders during the promotion. Then, as it looked like the Sox would make it to the Series and even win it, Jordan's took out print and television ads reminding people of the promotion and rooting the Sox to victory. Once the Red Sox completed the sweep of the Rockies, Jordan's made it very easy for customers to complete and submit rebate forms. The promotion was a classic rainmaker homerun. The cost to Jordan's was small, limited to the cost of an insurance policy; but the benefits were huge. Jordan's converted 30,000 customers into lifelong evangelists, won the affection of Red Sox fans throughout New England, and received millions of dollars worth of free publicity in local and national newspapers and broadcast news programs.

Jay Blacker and Jordan's Furniture have approached business in distinctive ways that suit their individual personalities and industries. The universal truth in their approach revolves around engaging customers and clients in a mutually beneficial relationship wherein marketing both makes the introduction and closes the deal with no selling required.

ROE #48

REDUCE YOUR ATTENTION SPAM

People do not have short attention spans. If they did, three-hour blockbuster movies, seven-hundred-page novels, and the weeklong build-up to the Super Bowl would be things of the past. People's attention spans are virtually unlimited as long as they're being entertained and informed. Attention spans diminish dramatically, however, when minds and bodies are being spammed by irrelevancy. Your job as a rainmaking marketer is to always be relevant, and the payback is that you'll always be heard.

Concern about short attention spans is a euphemism for lazy marketing and an excuse for weak content. Instead of accepting blame for spamming the marketplace with dreck and drivel, marketers lash out at the consumer. What they conveniently forget, however, is that even in this age of TiVo and fast-forwarding through television commercials, consumers regularly *choose* to watch compilations of the "best" and "funniest" commercials. People don't hate advertising, they simply and rightfully hate bad advertising.

Clutter is the culprit. We're inundated with information, sounds, images, and other sensory distractions, and it takes considerable time and energy to sort through it all and separate the good from the bad. And because there's way more bad than good, it can be an overwhelming challenge that is easy to walk away from. Our job, as marketers, is to make sure the consumer doesn't walk away.

Here are some basic principles to keep your attention focused on getting others' attention.

- More than one is none – As amazing as the human brain is, it works best when focusing on a single task or idea. Throw too much information at it and it will spend more time sorting and filtering than actively processing. If you want to capture attention and be remembered, you need to focus and get your audience to focus. Determine the one key idea that is critical and have everything you say or do build off of it. The more points you try to make, the less memorable any of them will be.

- A buried lead leads nowhere – Journalists get this idea pounded into their brains every day. Communicate the most important information first. The second most important information comes next, and so on—building the inverted pyramid that allows editors or readers to lop off the last paragraphs and still enjoy the gist of the story. If you bury the lead too deep into the story, presentation, web site, or blog, you may be the only one who reads or hears it.

- A strong hook will delay getting the hook – This corollary to not burying the lead focuses on the need to engage and intrigue your audience from the get-go. It's a technique used effectively by television crime shows when the first two minutes keep you watching regardless of how absurd the plot and/or dialogue is. You want to know what happens. You're hooked. So hook your audience early—but skip the absurd dialogue.

- Dynamism Can Create the Wrong Dynamic – Rainmakers tend to be dynamic speakers, but that attribute can turn into a triple-edged sword when empowered by the freedom of a microphone and a stage. The first, and hopefully sharpest, edge of the sword is your enthusiasm and your conversational, storytelling technique that will initially capture the audience's attention but, on its own, cannot guarantee to keep their attention. The second, and most insidiously common, edge is overreliance on one's own presentation skills—compounded by the related tendency to overlook the audience's needs and expectations. This combination leads to a lack of preparation that will be viewed by the audience as a lack of respect and common courtesy. If you don't pay attention to the audience when preparing your presentation why should they pay attention to you when you're delivering it? The third edge of the sword is the tendency to allow one's dynamic speaking style to warp into an unfocused stream-of-consciousness ramble. It's natural. You're an acknowledged expert in your field, and that's just the way your mind works. Unfortunately, that is not how the audience's collective mind works. Rather than merely demonstrating a command of your respective discipline, demonstrate some discipline. Get focused. Don't surprise the audience with unexpected twists and turns. Instead, apply the principles originally espoused by Aristotle in his still-classic *Rhetoric* and "Tell them what you're going to tell them. Tell them. Then tell them what you told them." If that sounds too formulaic, you haven't been paying attention.

- Losing the Crutch Will Stop the Audience From Walking – I love PowerPoint, and I'm a firm believer that, when used properly, it can dramatically increase the effectiveness and retention of presentations. The problem is that PowerPoint is rarely used properly. Instead of employing it as an illustrative guide that enhances content and context, most presenters use PowerPoint as a crutch. They overload the slides with words, bullets, sub-bullets, and pictures and then proceed to read them aloud. They use amateurish clipart, inconsistent fonts and layouts, and annoying transitions. In addition to insulting the audience's intelligence, they direct the audience's attention to the slides rather than the presenter. That's the route of wannabes. Rainmakers limit slides to a maximum of six lines of text with no more than six words per line. And rather than using the same old tired clipart that losers rely on, they purchase high-quality, relevant photographs for as little as one-dollar per image from web sites like dreamstime .com, istockphoto.com, or fotolia.com. It's fast, easy, and inexpensive—and will generate the right kind of attention.

Priorities Are Not

In addition to making sure to capture the audience's attention, rainmaking marketers also successfully manage their own attention spans. They don't maintain priority lists that number in the double digits. The dictionary definition of "priority" is a "thing regarded as more important than others." It is not a plural. Nor is importance the sole criterion for prioritization. Much of what this book preaches is that everything we do in business is important; however, if you view everything that's important as a priority, then nothing is a true priority and, even worse, nothing will get done.

The process of prioritization, and determining where to direct your attention, constitutes a balance between importance and urgency. Sometimes the littlest things become the most urgent—and hence have the highest priority. Conversely, sometimes the big things are less urgent and can move down on the priority scale.

Here's a useful exercise developed by Stephen Covey, author of *The 7 Habits of Highly Effective People*, to keep your attention focused on the right activities. Draw a square and divide it into equal quadrants. Outside the box draw a vertical axis labeled "Importance" and a horizontal axis labeled "Urgency." Write down your top ten so-called priorities and plot them into the appropriate quadrant.

IMPORTANCE	More important. Less urgent.	More important. More urgent.
	Less important. Less urgent.	Less important. More urgent.

URGENCY

If everything falls into the top right-hand quadrant, divide that quadrant into quarters and re-plot.

As activities are completed, remove them from the graph, but note where they were located. If you're completing more items in the lower left-hand quadrant, you may be more concerned with checking-off items as completed rather than focusing on the truly important activities that will move your business forward.

Pay attention to where you're paying attention.

ROE #49

CHOOSE THEM OVER US

Which of these scenarios would you prefer? Scenario One is to look in the mirror, smile at yourself, and say, "I am one good-looking guy." Scenario Two is to have a beautiful woman wink at you and breathlessly whisper, "You are one good-looking guy." In a world of too many complex either/or situations, it's a no-brainer of the highest order.

It's also a no-brainer that is exceptionally relevant to our professional lives. Consider which of the following would be a more powerful statement. Hearing a CEO say "We're a great company" or hearing an unbiased third-party say "They're a great company." Without taking anything away from the former, because CEO's by definition need to be positive and uplifting, the latter would strike a much more credible and memorable chord with virtually any audience.

Credibility is a key driver of success in every industry—which is why public relations is so important as a means of building and maintaining your brand, your reputation, and your business. Public relations actively involves the audience. It's not just about getting newspapers and magazines to tell your story, it's about launching multiple platforms from which to communicate your positioning and highlight the differences between you and the competition. It's about a new and different context for telling your story—as well as getting in front of a larger and significantly more diverse audience.

At its core, public relations pulls instead of pushes; and it inspires confidence and pride (both internally and externally). As such, public relations should be viewed as the vehicle of choice over advertising to build and maintain powerful marketing programs. Notice I said "should," however, because far too many marketers are far too enamored of advertising.

The more cynical of us might suggest that this fixation on advertising reflects the fact that ad agency reps always tend to need a fourth for golf at the local TPC course or just happen to have an extra ticket to the hottest concert in town. I prefer to believe that most marketers honestly don't know any better and simply travel the path of least resistance.

Advertising constitutes the path of least resistance because it's easier to buy advertising space than it is to earn editorial space. Advertising is a *quid pro quo* transaction—you pay your money and you get a specific result in the form of a print, radio, or television spot, as well as a quantifiable number of "eyeballs" or "impressions." With public relations, on the other hand, you pay your money (to internal or external PR folks) and you take your chances. There are no guarantees. Your company, product, or service may not get a single inch of coverage regardless of how much money you spend or how much time you devote to PR programs.

So advertising is clearly the expedient choice. But expedience rarely leads to effectiveness and is never an attribute of rainmakers. What does lead to marketing effectiveness is hard work, a clear strategic vision, creative positioning, and engaging storytelling. And that defines public relations at its best.

A public relations program is especially important for rainmakers in fields like law and architecture in which potential clients only become prospects when they have a specific need. Mass marketing would not make sense in these situations. Public relations, on the other hand, helps build your reputation and will serve to lead clients to your door when their need for your service arises.

Especially important to rainmakers is the fact that PR cannot be totally outsourced. Unlike advertising, where you can hire an ad agency to design the ad, write the copy, build the media plan, and submit the final artwork, public relations requires your personal involvement. The press doesn't want to talk with your outside PR firm, they want to talk to the decision-maker or the genius behind the story. If the PR campaign involves seminars or tradeshow presentations, you need to be the presenter—not some paid hack. People are the center of interest in PR programs, whereas people tend to take a backseat to products when it comes to advertising.

The moral of the "Choose Them Over Us" ROE is that PR allows you to enlist a credible third-party to publicly sing your praises. Interestingly, even when the third-party commentary isn't particularly complimentary to you or your services, you can still benefit from the PR attention. A lot of people believe that any PR is better than no PR at all. I wouldn't go that far, but I do believe that public relations creates a memorable context for your story—so the audience is more likely to remember your name, even if they don't remember the specifics of who said what to whom.

The big payoff from public relations is that—instead of admiring yourself in the mirror—you can be admired by hundreds, thousands, or millions of prospects and existing customers. And then when the CEO wants to motivate the troops, he can simply add his voice to the public chorus and honestly say, "*They* think we're a great company, and *they're* right." Perhaps that's why Bill Gates, the rainmaking chairman and founder of Microsoft, states, "If I was down to my last dollar, I'd spend it on PR."

A Word from Marketing's Undisputed Rainmaker

Philip Kotler, of Northwestern University, is America's foremost authority on marketing. He's also a big advocate of the benefits of PR versus advertising. The hardest part of marketing in today's world, he says, is having to compete with so many different media to capture people's attention. Because of its less intrusive nature and broader application, public relations provides a better opportunity to break through the clutter and be remembered rather than lost in the shuffle.

Kotler has developed a mnemonic to highlight the seven key tools of successful PR. The mnemonic is "PENCILS," which stands for:

- Publications – get your story published via press releases, bylined articles, op-ed commentary, letters to the editor, blogs, and vlogs.

- Events – use sponsorships, seminars, client appreciation events, and other public appearances to heighten your professional presence and reputation.

- News – position yourself as an expert with the media and serve as a go-to-resource for breaking news in your area of expertise.

- Community involvement – focus on networking and referral opportunities by getting involved in local groups and associations.

- Identity tools – continually enhance your personal brand via a broad range of professional development activities.

- Lobbying – take a stand on issues related to your expertise and work hard to make a difference. Successful professionals are expected to have an opinion and be thought-leaders.

- Social investments – give freely of yourself to contribute to the greater good and serve as a role model for rainmakers to come.

ROE #50

Just Don't Do Id

There's nothing wrong with a healthy ego. Confidence in oneself is a prerequisite of rainmaking. If you don't believe strongly in your abilities, no one else will either. Problems arise when one's ego gets in the way of an open mind, honest dialogue, and active listening. Rainmaking marketers fall down when they become overconfident. When they fall so in love with their own ideas and beliefs that they stop considering alternatives and block out what others have to say. Ego-driven marketing of this sort is doomed to failure.

No one cares about you, they only care about what you can do for them. That's been an oft-repeated theme throughout this book, but it truly cannot be emphasized enough. Id gets in the way a lot, particularly in regard to written marketing materials, web content, and client presentations. There's entirely too much use of Id-focused terms like "I," "we," "us," and "our." Often these words are used in an attempt to sound conversational and build a personal relationship. In reality, they have the opposite effect. They create an us-versus-them context and taint whatever information follows as suspect and self-serving.

No one understands this more than Nike. Between advertising and endorsements from athletes like Tiger Woods and LeBron James, Nike spends about $1.7 billion in marketing its wares. The power of Nike's approach is that neither the company nor the product is the focal point. Rather than talking about the performance-enhancing power of its athletic shoes, apparel, and sports equipment, Nike shows people competing, sweating, and pushing themselves to excel. The implicit message is that Nike can help you achieve your athletic goals, but it is never stated explicitly. Indeed, Nike's "Just do it" tagline has significant undertones of a pro-bono, public service message: Exercise is good for your mind and body and you should "just do it" regardless of whose shoes you wear.

Rainmakers can enhance their stature among clients by following Nike's lead. Providing advice and education that is product-neutral speaks directly to client needs. It positions yourself as a third-party expert who is truly looking out for your client's best interests. The systems analyst who represents content management software is far better off focusing on the holistic benefits of content management and sharing real-life experiences of organizations who have benefited from implementing the application rather than keying in on specific features and functionality. Similarly, an ERISA attorney can gain considerable credibility and goodwill by creating and distributing a mini-whitepaper on the impact of the Pension Protection Act and suggesting specific actions to ensure compliance—rather than calling clients and scheduling a billable meeting to discuss the same information. Certainly, the client can choose to work with another law firm to implement the suggested actions, but that will happen far less frequently than you might expect. When clients value what professional service providers bring to the table that perceived value goes far beyond billable time and exponentially beyond me-my-I-us time. If clients feel you're focused on them, they will focus on you as their provider of choice.

The simple rule is to check your ego at the door; but like most rules, it's frequently ignored. The most egregious example I've personally encountered involved the president of a mid-sized advertising shop that served as my company's agency of record. I was quite new to the company, and the ad exec was trying to wrangle additional business out of me. After trashing most of my predecessors for incompetence and for ignoring his advice, he began lecturing me on the various reasons why our stock price was low, all of which could have been avoided had only his voice been heard. I pointed out to him that Wall Street viewed us as a small-cap value stock—an asset class that had been out-of-favor for several years—and there were a number of future-looking initiatives and strategies that he was not privy to. He promptly chided me for having already drunk the company Kool-Aid, and I promptly began looking for another agency. The guy was smart and creative, but he could not see beyond his own pointed head. His perception was reality, and it didn't matter what anyone else thought. He seemed to believe that rainmaking was a unilateral process and the client just had to get out of the way so he could spread his genius. That attitude tends not to work for the client.

Just as the ad executive preferred to operate within a protective shell of his own making, inflated egos can cut off rainmaking marketers from the thoughts and contributions of others. This becomes painfully apparent when open door policies fail to lead to open-minded discussions. Many senior managers profess to want honest feedback but routinely discount it or reject it outright. They correctly believe that their lofty positions provide the broadest perspective from which to view and weigh the merits of various courses of action. They are incorrect, however, in believing that the broadest perspective provides all the information necessary to make a decision. It's that old forest or the trees dichotomy. Neither exists in isolation, and you cannot truly understand one without the other. Senior managers may indeed be "forest experts" but their staff of "tree experts" provides ground-level insight that cannot be ignored without enterprise-wide repercussions.

An overactive ego also contributes to the inability to admit one's mistakes and change direction. Far too many businesspeople equate mistakes with failure and, even worse, they view a change in opinion, policy, strategy, or tactics as a sign of weakness. Changing one's position has gotten a bad rap of late due to the disingenuous waffling that distinguishes today's politicians. In the business world, however, a quick change of direction can spell the difference between success and failure. Indeed, a distinguishing character trait of top-performing executives and rainmakers is a high comfort level with contradiction, ambivalence, and uncertainty. Their singular focus is on making the business succeed rather than continually stroking their egos.

The best way to keep your ego in check is to surround yourself with people like Christine McCue. Chris is one of the best public relations and communications people I've ever worked with and, God bless her soul, she never hesitated to express her opinions to me. It would take all my fingers and toes to count the times she walked into my office after a staff meeting or planning session and said something to the effect of "what were you thinking?" or "have you lost your mind?" or "you really upset me this time." Her feedback was immediate and specific. Most of all, it was welcome. Despite what my dog thinks, I'm not perfect; and Chris would often remind me of that fact. She kept me on my toes and helped change my mind when it sorely needed to change. Get yourself your own Chris McCue and keep making the rain even when it doesn't all land on you.

ROE #51

Suck It Up

A friend and colleague of mine was taught by his father that these were the ten most important words in the English language: "If it is to be, it is up to me." He had this saying pinned to the wall of his office and he used it to inspire every activity in his personal and professional life.

It's a profoundly simple statement that gets to the core of effective marketing, rainmaking, and personal brand-building. A brand is only as strong as its caretaker, its champion, its public persona—and that's you.

A great brand knows itself. So if you indeed want to turn yourself into a great brand—you first have to understand exactly who you are. And then make sure everyone else knows who you are as well. Keep in mind, however, that this doesn't happen overnight. It requires commitment and a lot of hard work. Simply talking about who you are doesn't build your brand or inspire confidence and trust. It's demonstrating who you are that makes the difference.

A lot of it comes down to something as simple as attitude. Think about this, for example. Suppose New England Patriots quarterback, Tom Brady, stepped into a huddle where no one knew him. How long would it take for his new teammates to trust him? To believe he was a winner? Probably before he even threw his first pass. Why? Because his behavior and his presence would inspire confidence. That's part of Brady's personal brand. And his confidence-inspiring persona doesn't end with first impressions. The more you work with Brady and the better you get to know him, the more confident you feel about his character and abilities. Randy Moss, the Patriots' outstanding wide receiver, observed that, in practice, Brady "works like a quarterback who's still trying to make the team." That work ethic and commitment to excellence creates a charismatic package of integrity and leadership that is hard to beat or ignore.

The good news is that there's a little bit of Tom Brady in all of us. You can inspire similar levels of confidence and loyalty by leveraging your natural talents and never letting up. There's an old saying that one's altitude is determined by a combination of attitude and aptitude. The critical kernel of insight is that we have to operate on all cylinders to realize our full potential. We all know geniuses who have bounced from one career to another, failing miserably at each. Similarly, there are countless "natural-born salesmen" whose overreliance on charm and talking-the-talk has gotten them nowhere. People are complex organisms. We're multifaceted and we have to employ all those facets to achieve rainmaker-level greatness.

On a similar note, Wayne Gretzky, who was the National Hockey League version of Tom Brady, once noted that, "I missed 100 percent of the shots I didn't take." Rainmakers make things happen. That's an essential part of their job description. Waiting around for someone else to score—or to close the deal, make a decision, take a risk, or whatever—does not inspire confidence. Leaders, by definition, have to lead. They have to make decisions—including tough decisions and unpopular decisions. They can't procrastinate, abdicate, or second-guess. They can't worry about making mistakes, because mistakes will indeed be made. Just as Gretzky missed far more shots than he made, rainmakers are not infallible—nor should they pretend to be. Humility is a prerequisite of greatness. Tom Brady never talks about his poise under pressure or the accuracy of his throws; instead, he praises his offensive line for protecting him and his receivers for running great routes and making great catches. Confident humility is an essential character trait of rainmakers. It can't be faked or learned from a book. It has to be lived each and every day. That's what Wayne Gretzky and Tom Brady do. And that's what elite rainmakers do.

No Down Time

To the casual observer, greatness often appears effortless. In reality, however, achieving greatness requires discipline, hard work, and a tireless commitment. Sticking with the sports analogies, Michael Jordan is widely recognized as the greatest player in basketball history. He was so fluid, graceful and dominant that it *had* to be a natural talent. However if Jordan's greatness were due solely to natural ability, it would be hard to explain why he was cut from his high school basketball team. The more realistic explanation for Jordan's greatness lies in the intensity of his practice regimen. Similar to what Randy Moss said about Tom Brady, Jordan pushed himself longer and harder than his teammates. By the time Jordan was drafted out of North Carolina and joined the Chicago Bulls, he could have lessened the intensity of his workouts and still been an all-star. No one would have noticed except Jordan himself, but that simple fact was all the motivation he needed to keep pressing.

The great pianist Vladimir Horowitz once observed, "If I don't practice for a day, I know it. If I don't practice for two days, my wife knows it. If I don't practice for three days, the world knows it." As a rainmaker, you too have a special talent that sets you apart and that requires constant nurturing. If you allow that special talent to wither, it loses its differentiating power and you become another nameless face in the crowd.

THE BIG Q

The key to rainmaking success is to stand out and make a compelling case for your product or service. If you've gotten this far through the book, you'll accomplish that by asking questions, listening, and observing. The key, and ultimately final, piece of the success puzzle is the way you answer the 500-pound gorilla-sized question that runs through the mind of every prospect whether voiced aloud or not: "Why should I do business with *you*?" As a rainmaker, your response must be powerful and succinct. Indeed, as a rainmaker, you need to put the question to rest before it is ever voiced and before it becomes a nagging doubt. This is where you truly have to suck it up and accept responsibility for your success or failure. In the vast majority of cases, the people who choose to work with your firm are doing so because they want to work with you. Your firm, product, or service is often tangential to the purchase decision. That may sound like a contradiction to the first sentence in this paragraph that points to the need to make a compelling case for your product and service offerings. The distinction is in the way you make that compelling case. That's where your character shines through, where your unique voice is heard, and where the prospect sees a glimpse of the kind of long-term relationship they would enjoy by choosing to work with you. Think back to the Tom Brady analogy. Does it really matter what play Brady calls? The formation and passing routes have no impact on his ability to inspire confidence. The impact is made by the way he calls the play, the way he communicates, and the way he carries himself.

"If it is to be, it is up to me."

ROE #52

BURN THIS BOOK

David Ogilvy said, "Rules are for the obedience of fools and the guidance of wise men." The same goes for the Rules of Engagement. As much as I would love to categorize the 52 ROEs as immutable, it would be repugnantly self-indulgent. The goal of *Marketing for Rainmakers* is simple—create a foundation for success by engendering a marketing mindset. "Mindset" is the pivotal word. A mindset, like one's character, is personal, multilayered, and unique. No two are alike. They may share similar thought processes, but the workings of those thought processes are affected by and melded with one's biological, psychological, and experiential DNA.

If you've gleaned anything from this book, I hope it's an understanding that nothing is sacrosanct (except integrity). Innovation and creativity spawn from rule-breaking and seeing what no one else sees or understands. Any set of circumscribed rules limit the scope of that vision. And following someone else's rules can limit the growth of your business.

Consider this example. Suppose you had invented a recipe for a new food product. You conducted an extensive series of taste tests with consumers, and the product received rave reviews. Huge dollar signs danced before your eyes, but you knew there was one more critical step before releasing the product to the marketplace. You needed to file a patent to protect yourself from copycat competitors. It was essential. It was what all the big boys with all the smart lawyers did, and it's what you had to do to play in the big leagues. Who could say no to that logic? The Coca-Cola company could and did. Perhaps the best-kept commercial secret of all-time is the formula for Coca-Cola. Known to only a handful of people at any one time and secured in a vault in Atlanta, the Coca-Cola formula has never been patented. Doing so would have made the formula public; and while a patent would have protected the formula for several decades, patents eventually expire and, today, anyone could produce and distribute a soft drink that tasted identical to Coke. And Coca-Cola, rather than being one of the strongest brand names in the world, would have diminished its cachet, become a commodity, and lost its ability to charge premium prices and demand preferred shelf space. One rule-breaking decision that still reverberates over a century later.

Creative thinking companies still flourish today by breaking the ROEs one at a time. For example:

- ROE #2: Be a Hobgoblin – GEICO has tossed consistency in the trash with its simultaneous advertising campaigns featuring such disparate characters as a British-accented gecko, disgruntled cavemen, and Hollywood has-beens interpreting the anecdotes of real GEICO customers.

- ROE #10: Feed the Lion and Spare the Mouse – PayPal followed the little mice tracks and figured out a way to monetize millions of small online transactions via a user-friendly, highly efficient platform.

- ROE #26: Don't Just Because You Can – The genius of Richard Branson is that his Virgin empire can expand and succeed in wildly different businesses. And while some of the new businesses fail, Branson, just like Babe Ruth, is known more for his homeruns than strikeouts.

- ROE #31: Speak Greek Only in Greece – Starbucks created its own language, forced customers to learn it, and built a community of in-the-know users.

- ROE #40: Choose to Lose – Amazon offered far more choices than any other bookseller had ever even contemplated, and created legions of fans (and happy shareholders) by creating a user interface that made browsing and buying a snap.

Most of the great innovations and commercial breakthroughs of the modern business world resulted from similar rule-breaking approaches—more commonly known as "thinking outside the box." Waiting for the proverbial "Big Idea" that will transform your business and the lives of your customers often involves an excruciatingly long, if not never-ending, wait. Rainmaking marketers aggressively seek out opportunities to twist and transform the ordinary into the extraordinary.

In *The Creative Habit*, Twyla Tharp defines creativity as "an act of defiance. You're challenging the status quo . . . [and] questioning accepted truths and principles." Rainmaker marketing is fueled by a similar contrarian-minded view of the world. Turn the basic tenets of your industry inside out and upside down. Look at them as though reflected in a mirror. Take the tenets, innovations, and defining characteristics of another, totally different, field or industry and apply them to your own. There is no shame in piggybacking on the creativity of others. In his autobiography, Sam Walton said, "Most everything I've done, I've copied from someone else." Walton is supported by jazz great, Charles Mingus who said, "You can't improvise on nothing; you've gotta improvise on something." The genius comes from the new applications and personal nuances that make the new version better than the original.

As I stated early on, marketing is not a department and rainmaking is not an individual. Similarly, rainmaker marketing is not a destination; it's a journey. The Rules of Engagement offer a map and some guiding principles, but ultimately it's your journey. Enjoy the trip and do it well.

Index